ADULTERY AND GRACE

Adultery and Grace

The Ultimate Scandal

C. Welton Gaddy

WILLIAM B. EERDMANS PUBLISHING COMPANY
GRAND RAPIDS, MICHIGAN / CAMBRIDGE, U.K.

© 1996 Wm. B. Eerdmans Publishing Co.

255 Jefferson Ave. S.E., Grand Rapids, Michigan 49503 /

P.O. Box 163, Cambridge CB3 9PU U.K.

Printed in the United States of America

01 00 99 98 97 96   7 6 5 4 3 2 1

Library of Congress Cataloging-in-Publication Data

Gaddy, C. Welton.
Adultery and grace: the ultimate scandal / C. Welton Gaddy.
p.   cm.
Includes bibliographical references.
ISBN 0-8028-4269-0 (pbk.: alk. paper)
1. Adultery — Biblical teaching.   2. Sin — History of doctrines.
3. Marriage — Religious aspects — Christianity.   I. Title.
BV4627.A3G33   1996

241′.66 — dc20   96-43368
                                                            CIP

Contents

PART I
A Hell of a Pleasure

PART III
Scandal of Scandals

Preface

"THAT'S THE WORST sin a person can commit," the woman muttered despondently. "It's unforgivable." A sixty-five-year-old woman had just told me of an extramarital affair in which she had been involved ten years earlier. Unlike most episodes of infidelity between marital partners, this one had gone undiscovered by either of the offended spouses. Thus, externally, the normal hellish fallout of a disclosed affair had been avoided. Internally, though, the affair had filled this woman with suffering. Guilt riddled her spirit. Grief had seeped into every pore in her soul. Depression dominated her emotions. A devastating sense of alienation from God held her spirituality hostage.

"What makes you say that?" I asked. "Why do you think your extramarital involvement was the worst sin a person can commit?"

A look of dismay covered the face of my counselee as she responded, "You know. It involved sex. I betrayed my husband. Another family was hurt. There is nothing worse than that. Nothing."

"Was it worse than murder?" I inquired. The woman stared at me in silence. So I posed another question: "Is adultery a worse sin than denying Christ?" The facial expression of hardened hurt on the woman seated across from me remained as constant as her silence. I pressed on, "Can you rank sins? Is one sin really worse than another?"

"Yes!" she declared. My last question prompted an audible response. "I can't explain it exactly," the woman continued, "but adultery is the worst sin a person can commit."

"Do you think God can forgive you for your adulterous behavior?" I asked.

After shifting nervously in her chair, the woman mumbled, "I suppose so."

"Can you forgive yourself?" I asked next.

"I really don't think so," the woman said slowly. "Adultery is just the worse sin a person can commit. And I am guilty of adultery."

The idea for this book had been in my mind for quite some time. My conversation with this counselee solidified my resolve to write it. The woman in my office was a longtime member of a church, actually a leader in a local congregation. She could quote Scripture verses about forgiveness and speak of grace better than most people. However, she could not see any connection between the grace promised by God in the Bible and the adulterous behavior that had played havoc with her life. This woman had done wrong in her affair. Worse still, though, she was continuing to do wrong by not accepting the grace that God offers to all people.

Unfortunately, the woman with whom I discussed adultery is not alone — neither in her thoughts nor in her misery. A bank dismisses an employee from an executive level position because he "cheated" on his wife and customers don't like that kind of behavior among executives. More than fifteen years after public revelations of her love affair with a government official, a woman continues to be identified by other members of her garden club as "that hussy who committed adultery." The religious "grapevine" passes along the word that a certain minister should never be employed by a church again because he is guilty of adultery. A man who has been through a divorce, which several different counselors recommended as "best for everybody involved," worries that a decision to remarry represents a willful, unforgivable act of adultery. Innumerable people needlessly endure prolonged spiritual and emotional suffering because they (or the most influential people around them) consider adultery to be a sin like no other, an act of wrongdoing that grace cannot (or does not) touch.

All too often, institutions of religion, notably local churches — ostensibly dispensaries of grace — compound the problems and intensify the trauma that plague people who have committed adultery. Ministers preach biblical grace, but practice vengeful judgment. Congregations invite "any and all" people to experience God's forgiveness, but turn away from their fellowships individuals guilty of "morals" charges. Undistinguished from other social bodies in this matter, the church tends to treat adultery as a sin so terrible that applying grace to it is unimaginable, thus demonstrating a scandalous misunderstanding of sin, adultery, and grace.

On the pages that follow you will find one person's attempt to call a halt to the graceless thought and behavior that so frequently attack both the subject of adultery and the persons guilty of this sin. I want to encourage people locked in a prison cell of guilt to exit this bondage by walking through the door to freedom that God has already opened to them. My hope is that the same material that helps individuals who wrestle with the guilt of adultery will also enable others, specifically those committed to Christ, to resign from their self-appointed positions as judges and jurors eager to mete out punishment and to take up the divinely commissioned work of grace as agents of redemption.

Even the best intentions to help hurting people and stir hope within the despondent have little practical value if the help is without foundations and the hope devoid of substance. So the work that follows represents my attempt to lay the foundations on which help can be constructed and to offer the substance that gives hope definition in relation to the issues of adultery and grace. Readers interested in additional research and reading on these subjects can find assistance in the detailed bibliographical material included in the footnotes throughout this volume.

Just in case somebody wants to know the bottom line of this book without working through the complete text to get to it, I want the book's conclusion to be known up front. A careful study of adultery — its causes and consequences — and a painstaking examination of the Bible's specific teachings on adultery and grace lead to a bifocaled conclusion: First, the sin of adultery is no greater than other sins in the sight of God. Second, to withhold grace and forgiveness from people guilty of adultery (or for persons guilty of adultery to withhold grace and forgiveness from themselves) constitutes a wrong equal in its severity to that of adultery.

If you consider adultery scandalous, wait till you really understand grace!

C. WELTON GADDY

Introduction

There may be as many acts of infidelity in our society as there are traffic accidents.

Frank Pittman[1]

I don't think there are any men who are faithful to their wives.

Jacqueline Kennedy Onassis[2]

TWO OUT of every three married men in our society commit adultery. So does one out of every two wives.[3]

1. Frank Pittman, *Private Lies: Infidelity and the Betrayal of Intimacy* (New York: W. W. Norton, 1989), 117.
2. Cited in Peter McWilliams, *Love 101: To Love Oneself Is the Beginning of a Lifelong Romance* (Los Angeles: Prelude Press, 1995), 358.
3. Accurate statistics on adulterous behavior are almost impossible to establish. Data analysts find that men tend to overstate the number of their extramarital sexual involvements, while women tend to understate or completely conceal the level of their participation in such relationships. Further complicating statistical integrity regarding the frequency of adultery are broad variations in survey methodologies: widely varying approaches to choosing persons for interviews, strategic diversity in the types of questions used to secure information, and significant uncertainty regarding the representative nature of the segments of the population surveyed.

Compared with other earlier surveys, the 1990 Kinsey Report contains the lowest estimates of adulterous behavior in the United States. This study suggests that 29 percent

Virtually nobody approves of adultery. At least most surveys indicate as much. However, a well-documented, pervasive disapproval of
adultery among the American public fails to prevent scores of individuals
from becoming involved in adulterous relations. Frank Pittman, a highly
respected marriage and family therapist, recently observed, "Infidelity
is so common it is no longer deviant."[4]

Adultery occurs among persons who rendezvous just off filth-
littered city streets and down bumpy dirt roads in small rural villages.
Adulterous sex takes place on a tattered towel thrown across the card-
board floor of a lean-to shanty in a dead-end alley and between satin
sheets covering an oversize bed in a penthouse apartment overlooking a
country club.

A public directory of adulterers (perish the thought!) would include

---

of wives and 37 percent of husbands were involved in extramarital affairs. However, data
from other surveys, many antedating the 1990 Kinsey Report, raise serious questions
about the accuracy of the Kinsey numbers. Several marriage and family therapists judge
the Kinsey figures to be extremely conservative, if not totally inaccurate. Dalma Heyn,
The Erotic Silence of the American Wife (New York: Turtle Bay Books, 1992), 26.

Citing L. Wolfe, *Women and Sex in the 80s: The Cosmo Report* (New York: Arbor
House, 1981), and S. Hite, *The Hite Report on Male Sexuality* (New York: Ballantine Books,
1981), Helen Fisher reports that 54 percent of married women had participated in an
affair and 71 percent of men married over two years had been adulterous. Fisher also
draws a piece of data from "Marriage and Divorce Today," June 1, 1987: "Seventy
percent of all Americans engage in an affair sometime during their marital life." Helen E.
Fisher, *Anatomy of Love: The Natural History of Monogamy, Adultery, and Divorce* (New York:
W. W. Norton, 1992), 85-86.

Authors of a more recent book estimate that 50 percent of all people have
extramarital affairs. Janet Reibstein and Martin Richards, *Sexual Arrangements: Marriage
and the Temptation of Infidelity* (New York: Charles Scribner's Sons, 1993), 4.

According to Sherry Hite's controversial studies, 70 percent of women married
for more than five years are having sex outside their marriages and 72 percent of men
married more than two years are not monogamous. Sherry Hite, *Women and Love: A
Cultural Revolution in Progress* (New York: Alfred A. Knopf, 1987), 365, 412.

The most recent study of sexual behavior in America, the National Health and
Social Life Survey, reports findings that directly contradict much of the data secured
by earlier surveys. Authors of this work consider most of these prior studies "method-
ologically flawed" investigations that produced "data unreliable, uninterpretible, and
impossible to use to understand sexual behavior." According to the NHSLS, the vast
majority of Americans remain faithful to their spouses as long as their marriages are
intact. "More than 80 percent of women and 65 to 85 percent of men of every age report
that they had no partners other than their spouse while they were married." Robert T.
Michael, John H. Gagnon, Edward O. Laumann, and Gina Kolata, *Sex in America: A
Definitive Survey* (Boston: Little, Brown and Co., 1994), 11, 16, 89-110.

4. Pittman, 13.

the names of chief executives of major corporations and house cleaners on temporary assignments, powerful politicians and nearly-bored-to-death factory workers, bank presidents and university professors, gospel-loving ministers and convicted criminals. Acts of marital infidelity occur among persons positioned at every point along the economic continuum, at every level of formal education, and at every stratum of social division.

Adultery spells scandal (in red letters) — whether in a family or a community, in a business corporation or a religious institution, in the halls of government or the glitter-coated world of entertainment. Whispered words of love give way to howls of resentment, disappointment, and bitter disgust. Private secrets explode into headlines placarded across tabloid publications. Fact and fiction merge without discretion. Rumors fly like daggers. Reputations rot. Jobs are terminated. Families break up. People get hurt — a lot of people are rocked by incredible pain.

HURTFUL HYPOCRISY

Not uncommonly, revelations of marital infidelity breed epidemics of rank hypocrisy. In public, people express their outrage over the behavior of the exposed parties and decry the shocking decline in morality apparent in society. Privately, though, these very same individuals feed their rabid fascination with adulterous actions by eagerly seeking to learn all the juicy details of what happened in relationships they have condemned. Balancing such disparate emotions allows folks to properly disdain guilty adulterers while vicariously delighting in the risque excitement of their affairs.

Projecting an image of untainted moral veracity, people lash out at a fallen woman in their community. Their language reeks with words of righteous indignation. A buzz of denouncements sweeps through a book club meeting, a civic reception, or a missionary support group gathering. But then come conversations about the arts. Denunciations of a fallen neighbor give way to lighthearted endorsements of recent books, movies, and stage presentations that weave together wild tales of adulterous acts. People speak of fictional stories of infidelity as "cute," "exciting," and "too good to miss."

Such hypocrisy would prompt laughter were not its consequences so destructive. A media mogul calls for the resignation of a popular politician accused of marital infidelity. She files her bombshell story of character assassination just prior to rushing off to meet her sexual liaison for the evening. In a local church, the board of trustees votes to oust an associate minister on its staff who is charged with "moral indiscretion" (an ecclesiastical synonym for an affair involving adultery). The chair of the board, a man who presides over the meeting with great poise and piety, currently enjoys a torrid romantic relationship with an employee in his office.

"What's the point?" you ask, before asserting, "Two wrongs still don't make a right. The evil of hypocrisy does not justify adultery." Of course not.

SCANDALS

Adultery is wrong. So too are the most common responses to persons caught up in adulterous relations.

Consider the extremes. While masses of moral crusaders take it upon themselves to inflict punishment on individuals guilty of "this gross immorality," much of society yawns. Both those who couldn't care less about what has happened and those who envision themselves as benighted emissaries of divine wrath are wrong. Adultery is far too serious a matter to be ignored. But adultery does not stand beyond the reach of grace.

Set grace and adultery side by side. Both are scandalous — adultery because it falls below a general moral standard and grace because it transcends morals altogether. Adultery describes a relationship in which a married person violates the covenant of monogamy and perpetrates infidelity. Grace means loving-kindness, mercy in action, which involves an initiative to bestow good on people who don't deserve it and who may not even have requested it.

Apply grace to adultery. Then quickly duck. Criticisms will come at you from a variety of hurlers. Ironically, most people prefer law over grace. Listen to their comments: "We need to emphasize duty and reward discipline. People who break the law don't deserve to receive anything good." Society applauds justice (to each her due), calling for a system of moral equity that doles out punishment for wrongdoing. People scoff at grace (to each according to her need), labeling mercy as idealistic at best and unfair at worst.

Adultery is a scandal — an act that offends the morality of a community. But grace is an even greater scandal! If you want to see a scandal of major proportions, apply grace to adultery and treat adulterers mercifully.

God-inspired grace refuses to allow sin, any sin, to destroy a life. Grace sets adultery aside — forgiving the people involved in an adulterous relationship; encouraging them to learn from what has happened; inviting them to use their errors, hurts, and sins as resources for service to others; and providing them with a future that abounds with new possibilities for meaning, joy, and fulfillment. Strong protests erupt immediately.

People bent on passing judgment, inflicting punishment, and expunging all evil from life suddenly decide that God is not moral enough. "We can't risk being soft on sin," they complain. "How can we support durable marriages if we go around offering grace to people who have been unfaithful to their spouses? The best response to any sin, particularly the sin of adultery, is hard-nosed, law-laced judgment. Make sinners pay for their wrongs." Even people who identify themselves as theists, children of God, and Christian disciples display a reticence to exercise the absolute grace that constitutes the essence of God's nature. Grace is a real problem. A scandal.

Scandal surrounds adultery. But the most serious scandal by far amid revelations of adulterous behavior consists not of what happened in private between the adulterers but of what happens in public when God's grace touches the lives of those people. Locked-jaw moralists decry grace, irate with anger. They find offensive and label as absurdly scandalous the very idea that adulterers should be treated with grace — God's kind of grace — goodwill, help, service, support, and love for the undeserving.

Graceless judgment (a non-Christian attitude) in a community results in a lot of people hurting badly because their very identities are defined by their adulterous actions. Seeking to move beyond the past, many of these penitent individuals find their spirits crippled and their efforts to get on with life impeded severely, if not completely defeated, by the words and deeds of people avowedly dedicated to "Christian morals." The very persons who should be most helpful to individuals hurting because of immorality stand as roadblocks *(skandala)* preventing those who hurt from moving on to health and wholeness. Self-appointed, self-righteous guardians of morality claim that an unwavering commitment to righteousness prevents them from even being kind to the unrighteous, much less offering assistance to those who have done wrong.

Why? Why does condemnatory, punishment-inflicting judgment seem more righteous than unconditional grace? Why must certain individuals attempt to be more righteous than God? And what is it about adultery? Why do so many folks view adultery as the epitome of immorality? How is it that high-minded individuals can tolerate, if not outright forgive, dishonesty, thievery, and even murder, but not adultery? Why does society attach the label "a morals charge" only to those sins that involve sex?

Adultery is a sin. Practically no one seriously debates that truth. But equally sinful are reactions to adultery that withhold grace from adulterers.

A FALSE GOSPEL

"Fine," you say, "we can always use another book on grace." Then comes a look of bewilderment followed by the query, "But why *adultery* and grace? Why not write about the applicability of grace to murder, lying, thievery, or just to sin generally?" Good question.

First, I have taken a cue from several writers of holy Scripture. Faced with the challenge of how best to describe the merciful nature of God and reveal the depths of divine mercy, numerous biblical authors chose to relate God's grace to the repugnant sin of adultery.[5] Israel betrayed God's good favor. Writer after writer likened this spiritual infidelity to adultery. Consequently, no one missed seeing the severity of the offense. Adultery was punishable by death. However, the point of the analogy was a dramatic presentation of the essence of mercy as well as a description of an abominable sin.

The God betrayed, the God against whom spiritual adultery had been committed, the God with immediate justification to punish the offenders by taking their lives, great God Almighty revealed the divine bias toward grace. And what a grace it is! Hurt by the infidelity of people whom God had embraced with a covenant love, God called for the adulterers to come home. Setting justice aside in favor of the sovereignty of mercy, God greeted the traitors with divine love and made them beneficiaries of grace. Far more than forgiveness was involved. There was none of that "I forgive you, but I want no more to do with you"

5. For example, see Jer. 7:9; 23:10; Ezek. 23:45; and Rev. 2:22.

kind of talk. Complete restoration took place. God extended full fellowship, as well as all the benefits enjoyed by any member of the divine family, to the adulterers.

A single occurrence of such mercy boggles the mind. Unfortunately, we are not accustomed to demonstrations of that kind of grace. But that is not the half of it. God's people flirted with infidelity and committed spiritual adultery time and time again. Adulterous actions took place not just once but several times. You would think God would have become fed up with the whole adultery-grace mess. Not so, though. Disdaining angry vengeance, God met every betrayal with mercy. People could not do too much, go too far, or cross any line that caused God to give up on them. Astounding! God's grace is as patient and persistent as it is endless.

That's one reason I have chosen to write about adultery and grace. Apparently no sin challenges grace and thus reveals the depths of grace more than the sin of marital infidelity. But my interest goes far beyond biblical expositions and theoretical arguments. What follows is much more than a theological apology for grace.

A staggering number of people suffer because of adulterous relations. Moreover, their hurt is often intensified by gross misunderstandings of both the sin of adultery—which is all too prevalent—and the grace with which God expects adultery to be treated—which is all too scarce. By means of this book, I want to take a shot at providing materials that can help correct this widespread misunderstanding of infidelity, challenge misconceptions that cause well-meaning people to confuse a commitment to righteousness with a refusal to offer compassionate help to the unrighteous, and encourage everybody to enjoy for themselves and to extend to others the gift of grace—unconditional, outrageous, often scandalous grace.

Many people continue to stick adultery into a special category of wrongdoing completely exempt from mercy. Folks willing to forgive almost any sin imaginable stumble over the idea of extending grace to individuals guilty of adultery. Maybe it is because sex is involved (to many people, sex relations outside marriage constitute the epitome of immorality). Or perhaps adultery's threat to the institution of marriage causes such vicious reactions. For whatever reasons, numerous people, even those (maybe *especially* those) within the church refuse to apply to adulterers the same sensitivity and compassion they normally extend to people caught up in other forms of wrongdoing.

Miserly withholding of grace from adulterers communicates a false gospel that is in fact no gospel. A graceless response to evil becomes another form of evil. To suppose that adultery (or any sin for that matter) stands beyond the reach of divine mercy, exists as an exemption to God's provision of absolute grace, and justifies merciless judgment is to entertain rank heresy.

If the gospel of grace cannot deal with adultery, it is too inept to cope with any form of immorality. If mercy is not for all sinners, persons obviously unworthy to receive mercy, it is not for any sinners. And everybody is in a mess.

So I want to bring grace to bear on what many people consider the sine qua non of immorality — adultery. Maybe an insight into how grace does its work amid the complexities of this specific evil condition will inspire commitments that cause people to live by grace in all situations.

TAKE HOPE

Untold numbers of people struggle with guilt derived from their involvement in adulterous relationships. Many of these individuals see little possibility of ever receiving grace from anybody. Sensing that no one else will forgive them for their wrongdoing, these people decide they cannot forgive themselves. Subsequently, their guilt grows heavier and despair develops, along with anger. Unable to envision a way for life to get any better, the spirit-broken individuals either lapse into a deep depression, develop a vitriolic cynicism, revert to endless sexual exploits as a means of escape, or just give up on everything and everybody (themselves included). They see no sign of hope even among people who speak of hope and sing of peace in services of divine worship.

That situation is as wrong as it is sad. And it is completely unnecessary. Despair does not scare away hope. God help us, were that not true. Grace fears no sin, adultery included. Redemption is always possible. Always! The future contains promise.

The Christian gospel offers hope to people plagued by guilt generated by an adulterous affair: Grace is for you — God's grace and the grace of God's people. Life after adultery can be good, maybe even better than it was before the wrongful act. Any word to the contrary stands antithetical to the gospel of Christ. Hear his message. Observe his actions. The idea of unresolvable guilt or a sin that disqualifies people from receiving God's mercy is pagan.

A PERSONAL WORD

A variety of motivations have sustained this writing project: I want people bent under the weight of guilt and blind to the possibilities provided by God's grace to experience joyful liberation. I want people who feel that punishment is the only right reaction to adultery to recognize the un-Christian nature of their thoughts. I want to exalt grace — God's grace and the grace that is to pervade every community of God's people — as the medium by which life can be repeatedly made new. I want to encourage folks to tear up their moral scorecards, be done with all thoughts of worthiness, and open their lives to the rush of grace that cleanses all sin and secures redemption.

My desire is that, after reading this volume, people who have committed adultery will realize that God's mercy is stronger than their sin, that divine absolution can remove every particle of their guilt, and that they can claim the future with boundless joy and a freedom uncompromised by whatever has happened in the past. I hope that some of the insights on the pages that follow will cause people obsessed with law and punishment and locked into an attitude of get-even judgment to stop playing the role of a vindictive deity and devote themselves to a life of mercy like that revealed in Jesus Christ. I pray that the words of this book will convey the touch of God's grace to all its readers — those who have betrayed marriages and those who have betrayed grace.

PART I

A HELL OF A PLEASURE

Bonnie and Kirk

Love is the child of illusion and the parent of disillusion.

Miguel de Unamuno

KIRK WHEELED his old Chevrolet station wagon into the parking lot of an all-night market. He had spotted a bank of three pay telephones on the dimly lighted corner of the building. Springing from his car like an excited teenager, this forty-three-year-old man suddenly forgot the fatigue inflicted by a long drive from a sales seminar in a distant city. All he could think of was making a call — getting in touch with Bonnie, hearing her voice, speaking to her.

A glance at his wristwatch startled him. "It's a little past ten o'clock," he thought to himself. "By now her husband is probably at home. Maybe I should wait until morning to call."

Kirk's argument with himself ended as quickly as it had begun. "No! I'm going to call. I told Bonnie she would hear from me as soon as I got back in town. Besides, her husband never answers the phone. I won't talk long. Maybe I will just let her know I made the trip all right and tell her I love her."

Kirk's heart rate increased as he rapidly dialed the telephone number that had been lodged in his mind for the last one hundred miles. His excitement mounted as he heard the ringing on the phone stop and someone on the other end of the line lift the receiver. Suddenly his heart skipped several beats as his spirit plummeted. A deep, gruff voice boomed

13

through the receiver Kirk held so tightly against his ear, "All right, hello."
Kirk had been ready to passionately exclaim, "Bonnie, my love!" He had
to muffle those words quickly and regain enough presence of mind to
hang up the phone.

"Damn! I hate it when that happens! Damn it!" Uncharacteristically,
Kirk was talking to himself. "That makes me feel so cheap and cowardly."

For the past seven months, Kirk and Bonnie had moved in and out
of a new world together. After a solid friendship between them formed
while they worked alongside each other as volunteers in the food-for-
the-poor program of their local church, each confessed feelings of attraction to the other. Long talks ensued. Every experience they shared,
like every word they exchanged, seemed to deepen their relationship
with each other.

Rubbing shoulders while shelving cans of food gave way to holding hands while driving a car. Conversations in the church building
prompted extended talks by telephone during every workday. Neither
could learn enough about the other. Each could think of nothing else
but the other. Both expressed a desire to spend more time together.
Kirk and Bonnie had fallen in love with each other, head over heels in
love.

One weekend, Bonnie and Kirk discovered that both of their
spouses had gone out of town. Immediately, the two romantics interpreted this unexpected gift of good fortune as providential. "This was
meant to be!"

Emotional bonding led to physical intimacy. Neither would ever
forget the evening of their first experience in sexual sharing. Bonnie
tearfully spoke of a freedom like none she had ever known before. Kirk
buoyantly talked of a will to vulnerability that was completely new to
him. Both confessed blissful happiness. And a tinge of worry.

"You know we just committed adultery." Bonnie broke a stretch
of comfortable silence as Kirk pulled his station wagon against the curb
in front of her house.

"Don't call it that!" Kirk snapped in a tone of voice that shattered
the crystal-like intimacy of the evening. Kirk's voice conveyed superiority, a one-upmanship in authority.

"Look, I know you've been to a seminary and all that, Kirk. But
adultery is adultery. And we just committed adultery." Bonnie would
not be deterred. "I'm not angry, my love. I'm not disappointed. I'm not
sad. In fact, I can honestly tell you that in my forty-one years, I have

never been happier than I am right now. But we must be honest with each other about what is happening between us. This evening we committed adultery."

"I understand," Kirk muttered apologetically. Then, regaining his composure, Kirk added, "You're right, of course, like you are about most everything. I just have a problem with that word 'adultery.' People associate it with cheap sex, superficial relationships, utilitarian thrills. I don't like it. That's not what we have. That's not what our relationship is about. This is love — the right kind of love, the best kind of love. The kind of love we share cannot be wrong!"

"Would you say we're having an affair?" Bonnie asked timidly.

"Absolutely not!" Kirk adamantly bit off each word, then incredulously demanded, "Why would you even ask such a question?" Calming his voice and speaking more sensitively, Kirk continued, "We are in love. We are sharing with each other sacrificially. We are committed to each other for the long term. This is not an affair. I really don't want to hear you use that word again. Ever."

Though Bonnie and Kirk continued to enjoy a variety of sexual activities together, a serious discussion about their relationship did not occur again for several weeks. The two lovers were disoriented by excitement, starry-eyed with romance, and fired by passion. But the inevitable next serious conversation eventually developed.

Concluding a telephone conversation with Bonnie late one afternoon, Kirk said, "Bonnie, I don't like saying good-bye."

"I don't either," Bonnie quickly confessed. "I've been thinking a lot about that lately. Real soon I want us to talk about how we can get together and stay together forever."

Bonnie's voice trembled as she spoke. Kirk felt an apple-size lump form in his throat. Romantic impulses shot through both of them, only to run headlong into troublesome doubts and fears.

As Bonnie's husband slammed the telephone receiver into its holder, he embodied disgust, "Some bastard hung up when I answered."

Bonnie smiled inside. "Kirk's safely home," she thought, "And he is thinking of me. What a wonderful man!" Suddenly, though, worry replaced her happiness. "This isn't fair. Not fair to us. Not fair to our spouses. We can't go on like this. Kirk and I need to be together. But how? We haven't had that talk yet." Bonnie feared that the massive surge of nausea that struck her was an answer to the question with which her thoughts had ended: "Will we ever be together?"

Bonnie skillfully hid her feelings, though. Nothing new about that. "Probably my boyfriend," she flippantly remarked.

"Yeah, sure," her husband snarled sarcastically, "I bet you've got a lot of them." Then, with a frightening eruption of seriousness, he continued, "You better not. If I ever catch you running around with another man, I'll make you wish you were dead. You are my woman. Mine alone! Don't you forget it."

Anger swept away the nausea in Bonnie. White-hot, scalding anger. In that moment, Bonnie hated the man who had fathered her two children. Doubts about her future dissipated as she whispered inaudibly, "I've got to get out of here. I wish I could talk to Kirk."

Late that evening, Kirk got into bed with his wife and immediately turned his back to her to avoid conversation — or anything else. Feelings that Kirk neither welcomed nor liked threatened to obliterate the incredible joy that had been his constant emotional companion in recent weeks. Kirk prayed that he would fall asleep quickly. But a question flashed through his mind and interrupted his prayer: "Do I have any right to pray?"

Across town, Bonnie fought off rough sexual advances from her husband. As she rushed out of their bedroom, she shouted a warning over her shoulder, "You better not ever try to touch me again. Do you hear me? Never, never again!" Bonnie tossed a half-opened sheet across a couch as her heart pounded against her chest as if it wanted to escape her body. She laid down knowing sleep was completely of the question.

The next morning, as soon as Kirk could pour a cup of coffee for himself and assure seclusion in his office, he phoned Bonnie. He breathed a deep sigh of relief when her soft voice answered, "Hello."

"Bonnie!"

"Kirk! I'm so glad to hear your voice!"

An obvious mixture of panic, sadness, and joy in Bonnie's voice bothered Kirk as he spoke. "Bonnie, we need to talk."

"I agree. We must talk today. Can we see each other?"

The two lovers hurriedly made arrangements to get together, and an hour later they met. Though Bonnie and Kirk had sat and talked in this same roadside park on numerous occasions during the past several months, today something seemed different. Stress creased Bonnie's face with deep, dark lines. Kirk could not sit still. He kept looking around nervously, finally admitting his fear that someone would see them together.

"We can't go on like this." Bonnie and Kirk spoke the words simultaneously.

After a long, uneasy silence, Kirk cleared his throat and started to speak. "I don't know what to do. I can't stand being away from you. Yet, I'm scared to death while we are together. I hate being apart. But I'm not sure how to work things out for us to be together."

Again, silence. Bonnie and Kirk drifted away into thoughts of other days. Everything had been so good. From day one, the relationship felt right. Melancholy blanketed Bonnie as she remembered early-morning phone calls from Kirk and surprising indications of his thoughtfulness. A profound longing developed as she pondered the excitement of a romantic rendezvous and, best of all, the unparalleled release of complete, uninhibited emotional trust. Her marriage had been all right. Earlier she would have said it was good. But she had never — never! — known a joy like that which had filled the past seven months.

Kirk reminisced about the very first time he told Bonnie of his love for her. A twinge of pleasure sent a shudder through his body as he envisioned the beatific expression that had covered her face when he said, "Bonnie, I love you." Then, there was the thrill of trying to surprise this remarkable woman, to please her, to make her laugh, and to be honest with her about his feelings.

The beeping horn of a passing car destroyed the magic of the moment. Both lovers jumped. The thought that someone they knew had seen them slammed the door on idyllic memories and sent the reality of the present moment crashing down around them.

Mystical thoughts of an other-worldly love stopped. New images appeared in their place. Bonnie saw her husband raving like a maniac, shouting, "You bitch! I know all about your escapades with that sorry skunk, Kirk." She imagined losing her home, her children, her security, life as she had known it for twenty years. To her amazement, she found herself thinking that maybe her marriage had not been so bad after all.

Kirk envisioned his wife wadded up in a fetal knot, sickened by the hurt of betrayal but energized by a commitment to carry out her vitriolic threat to make him pay for his wrong. How could he face his teenage daughter? And his elderly father? Kirk could hear his boss telling him to find another job. A sensation of loneliness, helplessness, and failure pervaded his being, seeping into the marrow of his bones.

As the early autumn sun climbed to the middle of a brilliant blue sky, Bonnie and Kirk continued to talk. But neither verbalized all that was envisioned, felt, and thought. They discussed divorce and mused over the least damaging ways to handle their children. They worried about hurting their spouses. Bonnie tried to calculate the extent of the scandal they would cause. Kirk named the friends he thought would support them and counted the number of people who would turn against them. Both confessed a fear that their church would condemn them and push them away from its fellowship.

At the advent of afternoon, each spoke angry words. Tears flowed liberally. Questions hung in the air without answers. Quick apologies abounded. But something was wrong, something that perhaps could never be fixed. A flurry of doubts assaulted what had once seemed to be an invincible certainty about the future. Neither Bonnie nor Kirk questioned the love between them. But both wondered if this love would last amid the pain that was sure to be involved in efforts to unite their lives permanently. Each sensed that the future held little that would be good for them.

A longstanding commitment to honesty forced the two lovers to translate their deepest feelings into words. At points, each questioned the wisdom of such stark honesty and wanted to renegotiate that commitment. Words like "guilt," "hopelessness," and "despair" dominated their conversation, words neither wanted to speak or to hear.

Finally, talk stopped. No energy remained to sustain more conversation. Kirk walked about ten yards away and stared across a row of picnic tables. A gust of wind created a shower of falling leaves. Bonnie sat atop a picnic table with her back bent and her head resting in her hands.

Both Bonnie and Kirk knew that the content of this hour served as a portent of days to come. Kirk walked back to where Bonnie was seated and stood over her. Looking up at him, staring straight into Kirk's eyes, Bonnie sighed, "I can't believe this is happening to us. Our love is strong. We are so good for each other. You give me so much pleasure. But . . ."

"Ditto," Kirk interrupted. Then, quickly turning his head away to avoid Bonnie's gaze, he mumbled in resignation, "It's one hell of a pleasure."

Love, Honor, and Betrayal:
The Dynamics of Adulterous Affairs

Thou shalt commit adultery.

The "Wicked" Bible, 1805
(Printer's Error)[1]

·AFFAIRS VARY in nature and characteristics, as do the individuals involved in them. Some affairs span a decade and take on traits of a marriage. Other affairs involve nothing more than a "quickie one-night stand."[2] Levels of emotional intensity in episodes of infidelity range from a "ho hum, just another escapade" attitude to a "once in a lifetime" commitment. Even the amount of sexual activity within adulterous relationships differs considerably — from minimal sexual touching among friends enamored with romance to virtually nonstop sexual antics in a partnership based on physical attraction.

Numerous affairs end as quickly as they began. Flirting leads to meaningless sexual intercourse and that's that. Other extramarital relationships, though, feed on maturing love and take on qualities of permanence. In a "matinee affair" (Helen Gurley Brown's description of a sexual rendezvous between two working people on their lunch

---

1. Cited in Philip E. Lampe, "Adultery and the Twenty-First Century," in *Adultery in the United States: Close Encounters of the Sixth (or Seventh) Kind,* ed. Philip E. Lampe (Buffalo, NY: Prometheus Books, 1987), 199.

2. Ten percent of extramarital affairs last one day, 10 percent last more than one day but less than a month, 50 percent last more than a month but less than a year, and 40 percent last two or more years. Few extramarital affairs last four years or more. Lampe, "Adultery and the Twenty-First Century," 183.

hour),[3] partners heed a cardinal rule — never take the relationship seriously. In a "secondary relationship" type of affair (Leigh's term for a long-term extramarital relationship with one person),[4] however, continuing the affair depends entirely on love and commitment.

No one profile sufficiently identifies the type of person most likely to commit adultery. It can happen to anyone, literally. No individual, like no marriage, can legitimately claim immunity to the possibility of an adulterous interlude.

Despite innumerable variables, affairs prompt two fundamental questions: What happened? and Why? Both of these inquiries merit careful attention.

WHAT HAPPENED?
VARYING PATTERNS OF ADULTERY

"I never thought Steve and Laura would face the crisis of an affair in their marriage." A woman in obvious shock was talking with two business associates about a couple who were mutual friends of all three of them.

"Neither did I," one of the men responded, shaking his head. "They seemed so devoted to each other. I can't imagine what happened."

"What on earth happened?" a worried father quizzed his deeply disturbed son. The troubled young man had returned home on a painful mission to inform his parents that his wife of ten years had left him after discovering he had been sexually involved with another woman. "What brought this about?" His father's words trailed off into silence.

What causes illicit affairs?

"Sin!" someone exclaims. Numerous people vigorously nod their heads in agreement. "Sin causes illicit affairs. People who commit adultery demonstrate evil's grip on their lives. They are bad people, immoral individuals, and they show it."

That is too easy an answer to describe adultery, at least categorically. Sin plays a role in adulterous relationships, no doubt about it. But

---

3. Jesse Bernard, "Infidelity: Some Moral and Social Issues," in *Marriage and Alternatives: Exploring Intimate Relationships,* ed. Roger W. Libby and Robert N. Whitehurst (Glenview, IL: Scott, Foresman, and Co., 1977), 134-35.

4. Wendy Leigh, *The Infidelity Report: An Investigation of Extramarital Affairs* (New York: William Morrow and Co., 1985), 59.

so do many other factors. Not all extramarital relationships develop out of a devious intention to rebel against God and pursue an evil course. Sometimes morally sensitive persons become involved in an illicit affair. The question of why affairs happen deserves further definition and more consideration.

How do illicit affairs develop?

What takes place in a person's life to prompt behavior characterized by secrecy and dishonesty? What power leads a man into acts of infidelity that betray the woman to whom he has offered assurances of love and promises of faithfulness? How does it happen? What makes individuals risk losing their families, the respect of scores of onlookers, and often their jobs in order to experience the pleasures of a marital relationship with persons to whom they are not married?

Wisdom allows questions of a general nature to be answered only with generalities. The best response to a particular inquiry about patterns of development in adulterous relationships involves a demand for specifics — "Give me a case. Who are you talking about?" No two situations are exactly the same. No one descriptive comment applies to the behavior of two different people. Given the involvement of complex personalities in a multidimensional affair, simplistic statements and popular stereotypes offer little help as interpretations of what happened.

Even when one is confronted by a specific incident of adultery, trying to get at what happened in the formation of the relationship presents major difficulties. One of the persons involved may explain what happened in a manner that differs substantially from the scenario described by the partner. Since an affair involves two individuals and both speak from an individual perspective, each may offer a "correct," though very different, interpretation of the relationship.

All generalities have exceptions. No generalization applies to all persons. Nevertheless, generalities constitute the best response to questions about what happens when an adulterous relationship forms. Developed out of careful studies of countless numbers of couples caught up in adulterous relations, here are four factors that contribute to adulterous actions (not the only four, just four).

It Just Happened

Ask several people to explain their marital infidelity and likely you will hear repeatedly, "It just happened." These words may seem as irresponsible as the actions that prompted them. In many cases, however, this statement gets as close to the truth of the matter as any explanation can get. Very few adulterers plan their infidelity. Confronted by an opportunity involving betrayal, they simply find themselves unable (or unwilling) to resist it.[5]

Fictional images to the contrary, most adulterers do not meet in one moment and in the very next moment hop into bed together. Typically, emotional or intellectual bonding between two people precedes physical union. In fact, each of the individuals may have sensed the stirring of romantic attraction and firmly resolved to resist any tug of sexual passion. However, cognizant of a spiritual kinship with each other, aware of great joy in togetherness, experiencing a new depth of trust in the face of mounting vulnerability, and maybe even finding unexpected unanimity regarding religious convictions, two people willingly give themselves to each other with a confidence and completeness that embrace sexual intercourse as a spontaneous act. At least at the moment, their physical union seems as right to them as it does normal.

"But if they are good, strong people — morally and spiritually grounded — that will not happen," a critic observes. Maybe so. Maybe not. Numerous studies indicate that religious people who regularly worship in a church or a synagogue are as prone to marital infidelity as the rest of the population. Their views on sexuality reveal a conservatism not shared by society at large, but their behavior differs little from the social norm.[6] Many experts in personal behavior believe we all have the seeds of infidelity within us. They point to individuals who desperately want to control the impulse toward extramarital sexual activity but get caught in an almost irresistible tide of emotion under circumstances that catch them off guard and overpower them.

Practicing personal responsibility when tempted toward an affair involves dealing with both morality and reality. Morality defines what *ought* to be. Reality consists of what *is.* An appreciation for morality fails to justify blindness to reality. Moralizing about a relationship rather than straightforwardly dealing with the realities of that relationship offers no help.

5. Michael P. Nichols, *The Power of the Family: A Family Therapist's Guide to How Families Work, How They Get Sick, and How to Turn Predictable Dilemmas into Creative Living* (New York: Fireside, 1988), 316.

6. Philip Blumstein and Pepper Schwatz, *American Couples: Money, Work, Sex* (New York: William Morrow and Co., 1993), 285.

Here is reality: Three factors directly contribute to the development (or avoidance) of an adulterous relationship—opportunity, strength of desire, and power of defenses.[7] Multiple other factors also, many too subtle to recognize, influence each of these contributors.[8]

Devoid of an opportunity for expression, rampaging sexual desires in two people may lead to nothing more than terrible frustration. Neither individual admits such passion to the other. Or a person devoid of the strength to resist temptation may be in a state of emotional disarray that kills sexual passion. The fact that adultery does not occur in either of these situations can hardly be attributed to exemplary moral virtue.

Change the circumstances of these people's lives, though. Have them meet unexpectedly in a situation marked by leisure time and guaranteed privacy. The sexual sparks that normally fly between them suddenly catch fire.

Opportunities for adulterous actions have increased dramatically in recent years. Rapid transportation and advanced methods of communication contribute significantly to the ease of indiscretions. So does the altered look of the workplace. In today's labor force, men and women work side by side, share long business lunches, cooperate on assignments, and travel together. A detective who has dealt with over a thousand cases of infidelity estimated that at least half of the adulterous relationships he observed involved coworkers.[9]

Given a lack of defensiveness against the drive of sexual passion (maybe for unrecognized reasons as discussed below) and a sudden unexpected opportunity for physical bonding, two people may throw themselves into an unpremeditated adulterous act. Looking back at the moment, the persons involved can be as surprised by their actions as others who find out about them later. Neither individual intended to violate the teachings of Christianity, to hurt a spouse, or to jeopardize a family. In a frenzied moment, spontaneity silenced the counsel of long-term convictions, emotions repressed reason, and desire superseded discipline.

"Aw, come on," a cynic snaps, "things don't just happen. People are responsible for their actions." False and true. Indeed, healthy people take responsibility for their actions. Sometimes, though, persons have to

---

7. Nichols, 316.
8. Frank S. Pittman III, *Turning Points: Treating Families in Transition and Crisis* (New York: W. W. Norton, 1987), 104.
9. Leigh, 59.

accept responsibility for actions that were unplanned, untypical of their character, and unexplainable apart from extended analysis. In certain circumstances, morally strong individuals become weak and sin. One can argue that such a development should not occur. But it does. When it does, the people's acts are unquestionably immoral. But those acts alone do not make the individuals involved habitually immoral people.

Watch out for a person who adamantly asserts that under no circumstances would she commit adultery. This is the very kind of individual who ruthlessly judges, condemns, and punishes people guilty of moral failures. Sadly, this person understands neither human frailty (from which no one is exempt) nor the power of situational decision making. Like Simon Peter of old, she promises more than she can deliver and makes boasts that her strength cannot sustain. She confuses idyllic blindness with righteousness and an unrealistic assessment of life with virtue. Sadder still, none of that will change until one day, again like Simon Peter, this woman, distraught over her own actions, sits in despair, saying to herself over and over again, "I can't believe what I did. I had no intention of that taking place. It just happened."

Falling in Love

Not all episodes of adultery occur as happenchance events. Sometimes individuals become involved in long-term extramarital relationships characterized by more substance and love than they found in marriage.

Quick conclusions about adulterous love are dangerous; it's easy to be fooled. Desires can feel like commitments and pleasures can pass as love. Nevertheless, occasionally, real love and authentic commitments do appear in a durable covenant between adulterers. Ironically, individuals can touch the moral quality of love in an immoral relationship.

Though it happens, finding real love in an affair is rare. The heat of romantic passion and the pressure to acquire physical satisfaction often cause people to lose sight of the nature of true love and the content of authentic relationships. Big problems and perplexing confusion arise as individuals define love only in terms of the initial excitement spawned by a new social partner or equate commitment exclusively with an uninterrupted air of blissful peace. Likewise, when people's understanding of a meaningful relationship includes only perpetual enthusiasm, lofty vision, tranquil agreements, and fun and games, serious difficulties develop.

Not uncommonly individuals fall in love with falling in love — not love for another person, but love for love. Much like a youngster frozen in adolescence, such an individual must always be on the exciting front edge of a new relationship. This kind of person moves from one romantic involvement to another, seeking to perpetuate the joy of falling in love. Easily bored, he never remains fully committed to one person alone (at least, not for long). Nurturing an exclusive love and allowing that love to mature simply do not carry the alluring thrill that characterizes falling in love. Count on it, adultery is virtually inevitable in the life of an individual who must always be falling in love.[10]

Important differences distinguish being in love with another person from being in love with love. People who need a lot of individual attention, who thrive on the spectacular, and who endlessly pursue ecstacy rarely find satisfaction in a long-term romantic relationship.

In any totally intimate relationship, certainly in a good marriage, negative emotions emerge alongside positive ones, arguments disrupt harmony, fears weaken hopes, and troubles demand concentration every bit as intense as that devoted to happiness. A less than mature understanding of love may cause disenchantment with a relationship in which tough adjustments must be made and heavy responsibilities assumed. Sadly, such an impatient, shortsighted view of love often rushes to the incorrect conclusion that true love no longer exists in that relationship.

Two people involved in an adulterous relationship frequently attribute their actions to falling out of love with their spouses and discovering true love with each other. Perhaps that is precisely what happened. Again, guard against a quick conclusion, though. Many impostors of love lay claim to deep devotion. Some people fall madly in love with each other. Others fall head over heels in love with love.

Sex as Hobby

Sex contributes to adultery. In fact, legalists often apply the term "adultery" only to relationships involving extramarital sex (and for them "sex" means genital intercourse). Marital infidelity, though, or an adulterous betrayal of intimacy involves much more than sex. As Jesus pointed out to his disciples in the first century, adultery can occur apart from sexual contact.

10. Pittman, 104.

Most affairs are not about sex.[11] Other interpersonal dynamics direct the development of betrayal. Apparently, however, some affairs are about sex alone.

Individuals exist who measure the strength of their manhood or the quality of their femininity by the varieties, conquests, and statistics of their sexual experiences. Recently, in a televised interview, a young woman described her fixation on sexual experiences with professional athletes, especially professional basketball players. She boasted of the high number count of her sexual partners and pointed to a closet filled with well over one hundred pairs of basketball shoes (trophies) given to her by men who had spent a night with her. This young woman sports enthusiast collects orgasms with much the same attitude as some people collect autographs.

Bed hopping is not always a matter of machoism and image, however. Not infrequently, a person who fears real intimacy (though the person may want intimacy desperately) treats sex as a hobby. An exchange of physical pleasure becomes a substitute for the kind of total sharing with another person that produces vulnerability, meaning, and durability. Having fun in bed takes the place of having to demonstrate emotional sensitivity, communication skills, and abilities in conflict resolution.

It's like drinking salt water to quench a rabid thirst. A person regularly engages in sex with a variety of partners in order to avoid the development of intimacy with anyone (especially the spouse at home). However, sexual intercourse, which is only one component of complete interpersonal intimacy, cannot satisfy an individual's craving for the whole thing — authentic intimacy. Thus, in addition to whatever physical pleasure occurs, a sense of incompleteness (and maybe sadness) follows each sexual episode. The person's chosen means for escaping intimacy becomes a powerful incentive to experience intimacy. A vicious cycle develops. A hobby develops into a habit. And this habit becomes a sickness.

Media talk shows laud men who boast of how many women they have "had" and glorify women who talk openly about the varieties of men with whom they have shared sexual encounters. In these broadcast discussions of sexuality, action-based words like "performance," "entertainment," "technique," and "success" replace more being-based terms

11. Pittman, 104.

such as "commitment," "intimacy," and "faithfulness." Such dialogues beamed to their millions of viewers and listeners remind me of a game — a sexual game in which the winner is the player who answers questions about how many, how often, and how different with the highest statistics. Audiences are titillated, if not encouraged, by first-person testimonies of how much fun can be experienced through sexual promiscuity.

A preoccupation with sex can become an illness. Sexual promiscuity can become a disease. Adultery can develop into an addiction as powerful as that induced by any drug.

Vicious Lust

Sometimes adulterous acts serve as expressions of anger, revenge, and/or rebellion. The object of the negative emotion may not be the person with whom a sexual experience is shared. A woman relishes getting even with her husband, who has caused her pain, by having an affair with another man, maybe one of her husband's friends. In other situations, individuals' vindictive emotions focus on the specific persons whom they seek to subdue (conquer or vanquish). A man with a near psychotic resentment toward women recklessly engages in sexual experiences aimed at hurting or humiliating each partner.

When motivated by vicious lust, sex is a means of power, control, and domination. The boisterous braggarts of sexual exploits tell the story: "You should have heard it, I made him beg"; "I wish you could have seen her, she wanted me so badly and screamed for me to stop." Such individuals identify their sexual partners by their genitals and interpret each sexual triumph as a put-down for the other person involved. Victors experience emotional highs by pushing their victims into emotional lows.

At long last, most of society understands rape as an act of extreme hatred and violence more than as an expression of sexual passion. Some acts of adultery belong in this category. Men who hate women and women who hate men often foster adulterous relationships in which reaching the summit of pleasure equates with plummeting their partners into the depths of despair.

Well, so much for the question of how affairs happen. Patterns of adultery vary considerably. Really, though, that's not the information most people seek regarding an affair. Concerned persons who inquire about what happened between two individuals in an adulterous relationship don't want a description of the sequence of events that brought the individuals together so much as an explanation for the events. "What happened?" is an interesting question. But the crucial issue is "Why did anything happen?"

WHY? CONTRIBUTING FACTORS
IN ADULTEROUS RELATIONSHIPS

Affairs develop from a mixture of motives. Circumstances that tend to move women toward affairs differ from those that act as a catalyst in the behavior of adulterous men.[12] Seldom can anyone isolate and describe the factors that contributed to a specific affair.[13] However, careful studies of countless numbers of adulterous couples yield a few documentable constants.

Here are ten factors commonly identified as major contributors to adulterous actions. These are not the only ten, just ten.

An Eroticized Society

Sex claims unchallenged sovereignty in the culture of contemporary America and wields the power to prove it. Consider the prominence of sex in art, entertainment, politics, marketing, and religion. A public preoccupation with sex bears witness to the eroticized nature of our society.[14]

Along with a pervasive dishonesty about sex among Americans, a fascination with adultery and the lure of sexual activity are facts. Americans endorse conservative sexual values when asked about their beliefs. However, these same people evidence a markedly different set of sexual values in actual practices.[15]

12. Carol Botwin, *Tempted Women: The Passions, Perils, and Agonies of Female Infidelity* (New York: William Morrow and Co., 1994), 33-34; Janet Reibstein and Martin Richards, *Sexual Arrangements: Marriage and the Temptation to Infidelity* (New York: Charles Scribner's Sons, 1993), 90.

13. Frederick G. Humphrey, "Treating Sexual Relationships in Sex and Couples Therapy," in *Integrating Sex and Marital Therapy: A Clinical Guide,* ed. Gerald R. Weeks and Larry Hof (New York: Brunner/Mazel Publishers, 1987), 157.

14. Reibstein and Richards, 5.

15. As a general rule, attitudes and values related to marital fidelity are not good predictors of behavior, according to Minako K. Maykovich, "Attitudes Versus Behavior

Americans exhibit ambivalent attitudes toward adultery. Most people label adultery as wrong. Yet these same people enjoy reading about adulterous affairs and watching television programs and movies saturated with adulterous actions, to say nothing of engaging in such behavior themselves.

Depending on who is asked, affairs can be viewed as acts of sophistication or depravity, attempts to avoid intimacy or efforts to find intimacy, evidence of a healthy sexuality or pathological sexual expression, and the antithesis of adulthood or the exemplar of adulthood.[16] Regardless of individual judgments, though, a social preoccupation with adultery prevails.

Dennis de Rougemont observed that a survey of literature points to adultery as the most notable occupation of both Europe and America.[17] Few novels written in the twentieth century fail to allude to marital infidelity, if not describe it with titillating details.[18]

Movie producers and television writers also contribute to the public's obsession with extramarital sex. Witness the widespread "would you or would you not do it" social debate sparked by the controversial movie *Indecent Proposal,* a film that told the story of a woman who agreed to engage in an adulterous relationship in order to make a million dollars. Television sitcoms, too, give short shrift to marital fidelity. Little wonder.

---

in Extramarital Sexual Relations," *Journal of Marriage and the Family* 38, no. 4 (November 1976): 694. Rustum and Della Roy write, "American culture is a living lie in its attitude toward sex: it preaches one set of values; it lives another." Rustum Roy and Della Roy, *Honest Sex* (New York: New American Library, 1968), 32, cited in Sue M. Hall and Philip A. Hall, "Law and Adultery," in Lampe, ed., *Adultery in the United States,* 85. Though persons who regularly attend a church or synagogue tend to be conservative in their beliefs about sex, their actions show no distinction when compared with the sexual behavior of nonreligious persons, according to the research reported in Blumstein and Schwatz, 285. Frank Pittman found that 85 percent of the public believes in monogamy though "most marriages are adulterous." Frank Pittman, *Private Lies: Infidelity and the Betrayal of Intimacy* (New York: W. W. Norton, 1989), 29.

16. David M. Schnarch, *Constructing the Sexual Crucible: An Integration of Sexual and Marital Therapy* (New York: W. W. Norton, 1991), 148.

17. Rose Marie Cutting, "Adultery in American Literature," in Lampe, ed., *Adultery in the United States,* 105.

18. Surely a broad-based fascination with adultery, not an appreciation for good literature, explains the astounding popularity of Robert James Waller's novel *The Bridges of Madison County,* a simple story of a brief love affair between a man and woman in midlife. Robert James Waller, *The Bridges of Madison County* (New York: Warner Books, 1992).

According to a recent survey, 51 percent of the top 104 television executives and creators in the United States indicated they did not regard adultery as wrong.[19]

Like it or not, social attitudes powerfully influence individual behavior without regard to what is right and what is wrong. Consequently, cultural endorsements of the attraction of adultery steadily erode even the stability of persons who enjoy happy marriages. Illustrative of the impact of social trends on personal practices, one research professional has concluded that presently, "within a sphere of working class, college-educated, middle- or upper-class married women, lovers are sought with a sense of entitlement."[20]

For a long time, sociologists have recognized the power of peer pressure — more people become involved in illicit affairs who have friends who have been involved in such relationships. Now, broaden the realm of application for that principle and the impact of socialization quickly becomes obvious. It's easy to understand why many marriage and family therapists point to cultural expectations as a (some say *the*) major contributing factor to extramarital relations.[21]

The Lure of Adventure

Studies show that sex with a different partner constitutes the favorite fantasy of most married women.[22] Men differ little in this regard. Set such a fantasy alongside intense speculation about possibilities for its realization and watch out for trouble.

Bombardment by provocative sexual images wears down almost anybody's moral defenses. Watching movies about exotic sexual pleasures, reading guidebooks that promise sexual ecstacy, and listening to gossip about friends ignoring the traditional limits of sexual activities can prod a person's curiosity about extramarital relationships and even develop a will for experimentation.

Tantalizing thoughts of sexual adventures alone do not usually lead a person into an affair. However, when added to dissatisfaction in a marriage or intermingled with other inducements to infidelity, the lure

19. Richard Zoglin, "Sitcom Politics," *Time,* 21 September 1992, 46.
20. Susan Ripps, *A Passion for More: Wives Reveal the Affairs That Make or Break Their Marriages* (New York: St. Martin's Paperbacks, 1993), xv.
21. Pittman, *Turning Points,* 102.
22. Botwin, 17.

of sexual experimentation can serve as the deciding factor in a person's choice to become involved in a sexually active affair. As one woman commented, "It's time for me to get my fair share of all this sexual fun I hear people talk about."

Some individuals thrive on taking risks. A risk that involves risque behavior packs a double whammy. Curiosity related to a risky, risque adventure often proves more than some people can handle.

Sexual Needs

For most people, great potential for an extramarital relationship exists apart from any outside inducements to sexual infidelity. The continuing presence of unfulfilled sexual desires in one or both persons in a marriage escalates into a grave threat to the health of that relationship. A powerful attraction to an affair develops in such circumstances.

A problem of unfulfilled sexual needs can develop in a marriage completely apart from either partner's intention to withhold love from or to inflict hurt on the other. Other factors must take the blame.

For example, a woman who associates her husband with her family of origin (a brother or her father) may not be able to experience romance unless she looks for it outside her marriage. Victims of incest and products of dysfunctional families often have the same difficulty. No one wants to "make love" to a sibling or a parent.

A man with a sexual problem like impotence may turn to someone outside his marriage in search of excitement and help.[23] Simultaneously, his wife may duplicate that pattern in an effort to satisfy her unmet sexual needs.

Marriage partners may possess appetites and attitudes related to sex that differ dramatically, if not work against each other as direct opposites. Positively, sex within a marriage represents love, intimacy, trust, need, happiness, fun, pleasure, creativity, and ecstasy. Conversely, marital sex represents negatives such as rejection, distance, hurt, evil, filth, and subjugation.[24] One partner may view sex positively while the other partner views sex negatively. The conflict assured by such polar perspectives frequently results in an affair.

Sexual needs in one partner often develop because of the chronic

23. Carol Botwin, *Men Who Can't Be Faithful* (New York: Warner Books, 1988), 108-9.
24. Humphrey, 156.

absence or unavailability of the other partner. Work may be the culprit, demanding long hours away from home on the part of one spouse, which results in severe fatigue when he or she is at home. Caring for several young children often produces a similar problem. The spouse primarily responsible for overseeing the children spends most waking hours trying to keep the little ones happy and most other hours trying to grab a little bit of re-energizing sleep. Virtually no good time exists for communication of any kind, sexual or verbal. The less tired member of the marriage, who feels deprived, may look beyond the marriage for a satisfying sexual experience.

Numerous studies document a strong correlation between people's permissive attitudes about sex as singles and their subsequent adulterous behavior after marriage. Individuals who have been involved in multiple sexual relationships before marriage are the most likely persons to engage in affairs after marriage.[25]

Emotional Trauma

Physiology does not tell the whole story, though. Many affairs, if not most affairs, result from troubled personal emotions rather than from dissatisfied biological drives. Generally speaking, participants in extramarital affairs are unhappy people.[26] More specifically, a majority of the people who become entangled in adulterous relationships are embroiled in a bitter struggle related to their egos.

Often the issue is self-esteem.

Red flags of warning should be attached to certain times of transition. During these periods, people become extremely vulnerable to an extramarital affair. Major transitions produce anxieties that gnaw away at an individual's sense of self-worth. Eventually the person seems to live as little more than an empty shell. Transitions force a change in assumptions about one's self and the world.[27] Engagement in an affair

---

25. Reibstein and Richards, 127.

26. Frank Pittman concluded, "Extramarital sex, when it occurs in a marriage that has agreed to monogamy, should be considered symptomatic, problematic behavior, and its specific meaning should be explored to determine what problem it is symptomatic of" (*Private Lies,* 28). In a much older work, Frank S. Caprio agreed: "Infidelity in many instances is a symptom-expression of some basic underlying neurosis." Frank S. Caprio, *Marital Infidelity* (New York: Citadel Press, 1953), viii.

27. Rona Subotnik and Gloria Harris, *Surviving Infidelity: Making Decisions, Recovering from the Pain* (Holbrook, MA: Bob Adams, 1994), 32.

represents a desperate attempt to feel important, worthwhile, and loved again.

The most common transitions that create the potential for relational troubles include a time of grief following the loss of a friend or a family member; the termination of a job; a serious illness; parental divorce; a serious failure; a bitter disappointment; a major change in status; and, for women, the birth of a baby.[28] These occasions demand adjustments. Subsequently, they set off unwieldy anxieties, which instill stress and inspire a search for relief, comfort, security, and affirmation in all the wrong places.

While some severely anxious people try to get better by taking a drug like Valium, others have an affair. Though it may not deliver on the promise, an affair seems to hold a boost for the ego, a reduction of stress and anxiety, fun, excitement, and a rediscovery of life. "Infidelity is one of the most common ways of trying to evade the severe emotional pain we feel when we face the emptiness inside ourselves."[29]

The more emotional trauma a person experiences, the greater the likelihood of that individual getting involved in an affair. Unaddressed uncertainties, doubts, fears, and wavering regarding relationships produce compulsive behavior. In the face of turbulent anxieties and disruptive fears, a compulsive person usually looks for a ritual to rely on as a tranquilizer. That ritual may be sex.[30]

Depression also is a problem. Repressed grief, anxieties, anger, and disappointments, or a lethal combination of all four, generate a grinding depression. As a person spirals lower and lower into depression, he may develop either the panicked sensation of a free fall destined to end in death or the passive assumption that nothing in life really matters. Either way the possibility of an affair takes on the promise of getting better. The excitement of extramarital sex seems like a perfect antidote for the heaviness of relentless depression.

Emotionally traumatized people seldom bring a moral perspective to their considerations of an affair. Involvement with a lover is not a question of right or wrong, a matter of wisdom or stupidity, but a chance to feel again, to experience something positive, to achieve an awareness

28. Bonnie Eaker Weil, *Adultery: The Forgivable Sin* (Mamaroneck, NY: Hastings House Book Publishers, 1994), 83-85.
29. Weil, 64.
30. Botwin, *Men Who Can't Be Faithful*, 75.

of being alive. As Block observes, for these people, the extramarital affair is not a luxury but "an absolute necessity as proof of personal power, vindictiveness, or reassurance."[31] For these troubled individuals, the affair does not represent a quest for sensual pleasure nearly so much as a desperate search for something to alleviate the terrible pain that pounds within every dimension of their personhood.

A Desire to Escape

Emotionally troubled people often view an affair as an effective way to get out of a bad situation. This longing for escape pervades far more adulterous relationships than the persons involved care to admit.

A variety of situations in the home can fill a marital partner with a desire to get away. After the birth of their second child, some women feel compelled to avoid being stuck with the primary identity of "mother." These women quickly move outside their families to prove they can still function effectively as sexy lovers. Occasionally a man seeks to escape his wife's pregnancy by turning to another person for sex. The presence of a problem child in a home often causes one or both marriage partners to seek escape through extramarital relationships.[32]

Obviously, a bad marriage can serve as a springboard, propelling its partners into other relational involvements. As Botwin observed, "A marriage filled with constant strife and unhappiness, or made sterile by an inability to communicate, is the perfect environment to sprout an affair."[33] Ironically, some participants in extramarital relationships actually credit their "flings" for keeping their marriages together. "Had I not had the affair," one woman explained, "I might not have stayed in my marriage. Without the escape of the affair and the pleasure it gave me, I could not have tolerated life with my husband."[34]

For individuals troubled by such home-related problems, involvement in an affair provides a way out of the marriage without ever having

31. Joel D. Block, *The Other Man, the Other Woman: Understanding and Coping with Extramarital Affairs* (New York: Grosset & Dunlap, 1975), 57.

32. Paulina McCullough, "Launching Children and Moving On," in *The Family Life Cycle: A Framework for Family Therapy,* ed. Elizabeth A. Carter and Monica McGoldrick (New York: Gardner Press, 1980), 179.

33. Botwin, *Men Who Can't Be Faithful,* 49.

34. Ripps, 31.

to say, "I want out." If the betrayed spouse does not decide to end the marriage amid an angry reaction to the affair, he or she at least becomes supportive of the other spouse's plan to terminate the marriage. Consequently, the escapee accomplishes the purpose without ever having to admit his or her intentions. It's a cowardly way to do it, but it's a popular alternative to telling the truth.

Not infrequently, individuals respond to jobs they despise in much the same way they do to bad marriages from which they want to escape. They engage in behavior guaranteed to get them fired once their actions are discovered. Psychologists refer to such antics as "ditching symptoms." Adulterous affairs are extremely popular "outs."

Professional people in particular are susceptible to affairs of escape. Once an individual has achieved a high-level position accompanied by a hefty income, it is difficult to admit misery. No one will understand. Stepping down from such an office and moving away from such a salary defy common wisdom. So the person decides to engage in behavior sure to result in a release from the despised professional duties. Though this resolve is usually subconscious, it is almost always effective. Some people embezzle money, others ruin their health, some create management problems, and still others have affairs.

Unrealistic Expectations about Marriage

Adultery cannot exist without marriage. That does not mean marriage causes adultery. However, unachievable expectations about marriage contribute significantly to the personal psyche and marital condition that inspire or tolerate an interest in adultery.

Many people in our society marry with expectations that their spouse can meet all their needs — emotional support, sexual fulfillment, intellectual challenge, and personal happiness. In fact, most marriage ceremonies require the bride and groom to promise as much to each other. It won't happen. It can't happen. No one person can bear total responsibility for the emotional happiness of another person, not even in a marriage. To expect such an all-fulfilling relationship in marriage leads to major disappointments. And that is only the beginning of the disillusionment likely to develop.

Society peddles mixed signals about marriage, commending exclusivity and permanence to prospective marital partners. Yet a study of the society that offers that commendation leads one to the conclusion that exclusivity and permanence in a marriage are incompatible.[35] Grave discrepancies divide society's promises about marriage from realities in marriage.

Nobody really wants to be unfaithful to a spouse.[36] However, everybody wants to be part of a happy marriage. Convinced by society that all other marriages are happy, a person in an unhappy marriage resolves to find a relationship that more nearly provides all that has been expected. More often than not, an extramarital affair ensues.

Hurtful Myths

Certain expectations about marriage prove to be as detrimental as they are mythological. The "marriage-is-for-everything" concept heads the list of such thoughts. That ideal contains within it the seeds of its own destruction. No marriage turns out to be perfectly companionate, egalitarian, and romantic. Marriage embraces too many different dimensions in which a breakdown can occur or a problem arise. Persons who expected marriage to be all they ever wanted or needed tend to be prime candidates for an extramarital affair.

Another myth that negatively impacts the reality of marriage asserts that husbands and wives grow to love each other more and more with each passing year.[37] Actually, that may happen, but it will not happen automatically. Growth in love requires work in the areas of communication skills, relational sensitivity, sexual expression, and forgiveness, as well as renewed commitments. Not to give attention to these concerns and yet to expect a maturation and continuation of love within a marriage sets one up for the kind of disappointment that, like a cannon, shoots a person into another relationship.

Damaging also is the myth that sexual exclusivity comes easily and naturally for people who are married. It does not. Most students of humankind argue that sexual fidelity between two persons is never easy or natural, that we are varietists by nature.[38] "Lifelong sexual fidelity is neither biologically nor psychologically natural to the human being."[39]

---

35. Bernard, 131.

36. Reibstein and Richards, 4.

37. Lynn Atwater, *The Extramarital Connection* (New York: Irvington Publications, 1982), 18.

38. Block, 59.

39. Morton Hunt, *The Affair: A Portrait of Extra-Marital Love in Contemporary America* (New York: World Publishing Co., 1969), 282.

Marriage partners who buy into the myth of easy fidelity and thus take an exclusive sexual commitment to each other for granted expose their relationship to a grave danger, making it easy for one or both of them to exit the family in search of new sexual experiences.

Crucial Transitions

Changes in a marriage occur whether or not the people involved are ready. A lack of preparation for major transitions in marriage contributes substantially to the potential for an affair, as substantially as do popular myths about marriage.[40]

In the early years of a marriage, each partner's previous sexual experiences (or lack of them) significantly influence their expectations and behavior. Major differences between two people's premarital experiences present a potential problem to a new couple, a problem that can drive the more sexually experienced member of the marriage to seek compatibility outside the marriage or can cause the less sexually experienced member to feel jealous of his or her partner's wider experience or wonder what he or she has missed. Later on, after children arrive, marital partners often need a new confirmation of their sexuality — a recognition of their sexual appeal and a demonstration of their ability to provide sexual pleasure. If members of a married couple do not provide this reaffirmation of sexuality for one another, one of them may search for it elsewhere.[41] More potential problems of this nature surface when the last child leaves home. After many years, spouses find themselves together alone again. This can be a time of celebration, a rediscovery of sexual freedom within the marriage, and relational growth for a couple — or a period in which spouses discover their alienation from each other and bolt into a relationship with someone else.[42]

Marriages have to negotiate major times of transition in much the same manner that individuals do. Careful and cooperative attentiveness to demands for change can bring a couple closer together and strengthen their relationship. On the other hand, failure to address transitions openly and honestly can create emotional distance between a couple and even send one or both of them in search of another relationship.

40. Reibstein and Richards, 113-17.
41. Jack O. Bradt, "The Family With Young Children," in Carter and McGoldrick, eds., *The Family Life Cycle*, 131.
42. McCullough, 179.

Rebellion and Revenge

Marital relationships can deteriorate to the point that one partner resolves to rebel against the other or, worse still, to inflict hurt on the other. Thankfully, instances of revenge are less common than acts of rebellion. The severe circumstances that incite revenge appear in marriages less frequently than attitudes and actions that prompt rebellion.

Revenge implies a desire to hurt someone. Sensing that the person to whom you are married cares only about your money, repeatedly reeling under public put-downs from your spouse, or losing all feelings of self-worth because of a constant barrage of criticism from your marital mate can spark relationships of revenge.[43] A man declares, "I have taken all the grief I intend to take from that woman. I'm going to give her a taste of her own medicine, and I'm going to have fun doing it."

Statistically, most affairs of revenge result from the discovery of a spouse's affair. Many people consider a revenge affair a far worse offense than the affair that caused it. The reacting party knew firsthand the kind of pain inflicted by a spouse's affair and decided to proceed with a revenge affair anyway.[44]

Unlike affairs of revenge, which develop out of obviously troubled marriages, affairs of rebellion occur in marriages that give every evidence of stability. As a matter of fact, the target of the rebellion may be something in the adulterer's psyche that does not even involve the spouse. In the context of a happy marriage, for example, a partner can act out resentful rebellion toward his family of origin because of the narrow, puritanical code to which his parents subjected him. "What could be worse (or better) than an extramarital affair to make the point that I am no longer under their pious thumbs."

A stable marriage can form the backdrop for an affair prompted by rebellion against the idea of marriage itself. "I love my husband, but my marriage to him has forced me to give up all the pleasures of life as a single adult."

Some radical feminists point to affairs as a welcome indication of much-needed female initiatives. "Those who seek the full-time lover strike the boldest pose of any."[45]

---

43. Botwin, *Men Who Can't Be Faithful,* 110-11.
44. Reibstein and Richards, 128.
45. Ripps, 233.

When circumstances force a person to mature too quickly, that individual may develop a deep resentment over the loss of his youth. Out of that resentment comes a decision to claim what he missed. "I want another shot at the dreams and pleasures that I had to give up in my youth."

A spouse's annoying behavior can spawn an affair of rebellion. Take a woman who must constantly deal with a controlling, depriving husband. Eventually she decides that the only leverage she has to get back at him is involvement in an extramarital relationship. "I'll show him," she resolves, first scowling, then smiling. Similarly, instead of dealing directly with the resentment he feels toward his wife, a man may denounce his spouse by having an affair.[46]

All kinds of problems accompany affairs motivated by rebellion and revenge. Often they result in a poor choice of an affair partner. The rebellious person may even feel great ambivalence toward his new lover — cherishing her in one moment and disliking or disapproving of her the next moment.[47] Anger mushrooms into rage as the rebellious individual denies the presence of any sexual desire for his affair partner and then helplessly gives in to that desire. His anger turns inward as well as outward, producing disdain toward himself, his new lover, and his spouse.

Family Influences

A growing body of research points to adulterous behavior as the sad consequence of problems in a person's family history. Bonnie Eaker Weil argues convincingly that most acts of infidelity represent an individual's effort to compensate for hurts, frustrations, and unmet needs in his or her childhood and youth. "People who are not in some kind of pain do not commit adultery," according to Weil.[48]

Parental influence is powerful, no question about that. "The basic foundation of the sexual script is laid in our early development through our attachment and bonding with our primary care givers," who are usually members of our family of origin.[49] Relating to our parents as

46. Ripps, 233.
47. Hunt, 171-72.
48. Weil, xxi.
49. Luciana L'Abate and William C. Talmadge, "Love, Intimacy, and Sex," in Weeks and Hof, eds., *Integrating Sex and Marital Therapy*, 24. L'Abate and Talmadge understand love as a developmental process involving three elements: first, behavioral

young children, we become conditioned to a certain quality of affection and attachment. This orientation, then, shapes our understanding of intimacy and impacts all our future relationships (unless it is challenged and changed). Persons who experienced fulfilling love in childhood know that kind of love is possible, search for it, and work at it. Those who did not know such love crave it while seriously doubting its possibility.

The stability of one's family of origin also contributes to the health or illness of that person's marriage. Because of divergent backgrounds, one adult may cling to a marriage, fearing the horrors of a possible breakup, while another pursues a series of affairs, scared to death of the downside of monogamy.

In her practice as a family therapist, Weil found that in nine out of ten cases at least one partner in an adulterous relationship was the adult child of an adulterer (some situations involved as many as four generations). Weil concluded that adultery involves an emotional dynamic that is transferred to children. Thus, the "multigenerational plague" of adultery often stems from an inherited behavior pattern within a family, not from the free choice of an individual.[50]

Midlife Crazies

So many jokes have been made about the midlife crisis that some people no longer take this phenomenon seriously. That's a mistake. The potential for a relational crisis in the middle years of a person's life is an indisputable reality. Statistics show that men in the age range from thirty-seven to thirty-nine and women at the age of thirty-five or thirty-six are the people most likely to have an affair.[51]

Why? What happens in the middle years of life that makes persons so itchy for involvement in an extramarital relationship?

Developmentally, this is the period in which most men struggle with issues like lost dreams, a protruding stomach, gray hair, a stalled

---

components — received care and caring; second, cognitive components — seeing the good and forgiveness; and third, an emotional component — intimacy (27).

50. Weil, xx, 10.

51. Botwin, *Men Who Can't Be Faithful,* 45; Botwin, *Tempted Women,* 26. For additional insights into the relationship between midlife dilemmas and extramarital affairs, see also Nancy Mayer, *The Male Mid-Life Crisis: Fresh Starts After Forty* (New York: New American Library, 1978), and Gail Sheehy, *Passages: Predictable Crises of Adult Life* (New York: Bantam Books, 1977).

career, and the departure of youth.[52] Often middle-aged men feel that they are missing out on life and want to experience more than they know. An affair promises just what they need — the excitement, risk, and invigoration that they long for.

For women, middle age is a time for honest assessments regarding their relationships. A discovery of disillusionment and discontent related to their marriages is not uncommon. Consequently, some middle-aged women enter an affair hoping to rekindle important old feelings and to rediscover a meaningful relationship that is both friendly and romantic.

Both men and women first seriously face their mortality during their middle years. A recognition of life's most enduring and important realities throws into question many of the endeavors to which they have devoted huge expenditures of time and energy. Facing the emptiness of professional success, losses that have been required along the way, and the attraction of intimate relationships, a deep sadness, if not real depression, develops. Living in and by love suddenly seems more important than anything else. Sensing that they have not experienced such love in their marriages or that they have lost it if it was once there, they find the lure of an affair irresistible.

Logic cannot touch the passionate love, or the surging emotions that feel like love, that develops in a midlife affair. The need to be in love and the satisfaction of being in love surpass everything else of value. Behavior patterns typical of teenagers appear.

Crazy things happen, often the crazier the better for those involved. Individuals may risk the loss of everything they have spent their lives seeking to attain by throwing themselves into relationships that make no sense and avowing a love that defies all reason. Hormones that they feared were fully spent pump through their glands again. They experience an emotional high like nothing they have ever known before. Feeling pride and looking foolish go hand in hand. Extramarital involvements among many middle-aged people represent misguided attempts to cheer themselves up.[53] And it works. Ecstatic happiness erupts. Life seems great, at least for a while.

Reasoning with persons dazed by such impassioned joy is out of

---

52. Botwin, *Men Who Can't Be Faithful*, 116-18.

53. Botwin, *Men Who Can't Be Faithful*, 116-18; Robert Lee and Marjorie Casebier, *The Spouse Gap: Weathering the Marriage Crisis during Middlescence* (Nashville: Abingdon Press, 1971), 159.

the question. Attempts to subject their affair to logical evaluative criteria fail. Appeals to long-term commitments in other relationships fall on deaf ears. As one therapist points out, "Marriage is unworkable for people who must be in-love at all times."[54]

The Intimacy Thing

Feelings about intimacy — either the desire for it or a fear of it — play a major role in most affairs. In an intimate relationship, both parties are in touch with their innermost selves as well as with each other, and are free to be themselves. "Neither party silences, sacrifices, or betrays the self and each party expresses strength and vulnerability, weakness and competence in a balanced way."[55] Achieving intimacy within a relationship involves two people arriving at and freely expressing profound self-understanding in each other's presence and with each other's blessing.

Some people fear intimacy. An aversion to any intimate relationship can result from growing up with parents who were not close, the loss of a parent during early childhood, a poor self-image that recoils from opportunities for self-understanding and self-revelation, a fear of suffocation by someone else's closeness, or a dread of becoming dependent on another individual.[56] People afraid of intimacy steer clear of relationships in which they might lose control, be expected to reveal a weakness in their lives, become vulnerable, risk rejection or abandonment, or be made the target of anger. Individuals who possess such a fear will do almost anything to avoid closeness even with the persons they love.

Ironically, for people paranoid about intimacy, the potential for an extramarital relationship increases in direct proportion to the good health of their marriage. The more closeness they develop with their spouses, the

54. Pittman, *Turning Points,* 104.

55. Harriet Goldhor Lerner, *The Dance of Intimacy: A Woman's Guide to Courageous Acts of Change in Key Relationships* (New York: Harper & Row, 1989), 3. Thomas Patrick Malone and Patrick Thomas Malone trace the derivation of intimacy from the Latin *intima,* which means "inner" or "innermost." They see *intimate* as an adjective that means "personal," "private," "detailed," "deep," or "innermost"; as a noun describing a close friend; and as a verb that means "to make known indirectly" or "to hint at." The Malones conclude that "This sense of touching our innermost core is the essence of intimacy: It contains all the qualities implied in its various definitions." Thomas Patrick Malone and Patrick Thomas Malone, *The Art of Intimacy* (New York: Prentice Hall Press, 1987), 19.

56. Botwin, *Men Who Can't Be Faithful,* 139-40.

more likely they are to make a mad dash toward someone else. As Schnarch explains, "When the goal is to be seen as you want, but not known as you are, marriage can never compete with part-time romance."[57]

By far, though, more people enter affairs looking for intimacy than fleeing from intimacy. According to Frank Pittman, affairs are three times more likely to arise from "the pursuit of a buddy than the pursuit of a better orgasm."[58] A few students of interpersonal relationships suggest that virtually all women enter affairs in search of intimacy.[59] But the pursuit of intimacy is not exclusively a feminine endeavor.

In an intimate relationship, each partner participates with ego strength, possesses power, and enjoys interdependence.[60] Both members of a couple strive for a vulnerability built on self-understanding and a will to share the self that is known. Frequent touching between the partners signals externally the mutuality and trust that are developing between them internally.

A lack of intimacy within a marriage greatly enhances the likelihood that a person will pursue intimacy outside the marriage. Deprived of opportunities to talk about fears, needs, hopes, and dreams and to make sexual requests, an individual feels powerless, alienated, unfulfilled, discouraged, maybe even desperate. "The extramarital affair develops as a way of finding a comforter and ally."[61]

A discovery of intimacy after a deprivation of intimacy results in great fulfillment and sparks incredible joy. Achieving intimacy in a marriage brings stability and happiness to the relationship. Experiencing intimacy in an affair almost surely spells doom for the marriages of the people in the affair. Seldom will a person who has experienced authentic intimacy choose to walk away from it.

57. Schnarch, 371.

58. Pittman, *Private Lies,* 122. John M. Lewis agrees, describing the search for intimacy as "the simple yearning to be close and to be understood." John M. Lewis, *How's Your Family? A Guide to Identifying Your Family's Strengths and Weaknesses* (New York: Brunner/Mazel, 1979), 83.

59. Shere Hite reports that most women in her study "are having affairs because they are looking for emotional closeness and support, a way to have a more real relationship." Hite targets "women's emotionally alienated state within marriage" as the cause of their search for love and enjoyment outside of marriage. Shere Hite, *Women and Love: A Cultural Revolution in Progress* (New York: Alfred A. Knopf, 1987), 409.

60. L'Abate and Talmadge, 29.

61. Maggie Scarf, *Intimate Partners: Patterns in Love and Marriage* (New York: Random House, 1987), 133.

A Mixed Bag

Rarely does a single factor explain the emergence of an extramarital relationship. Most affairs are multimotivated and very complicated.

Seldom, too, does an affair develop as an intentional act of sin. Adultery is a sin to be sure. But I know of no one who has engaged in an adulterous act for the specific purpose of committing a sin.

Numerous contributing factors combine to catapult people into extramarital relationships. It can happen to anybody. Many individuals guilty of adultery remember a time in their lives when they denied even the possibility of their involvement in an affair.

Here is what's really scary. According to Morton Hunt, "The temptation that first overpowers conscience, fear, and other defenses is likely to be both convenient and unsought."[62]

62. Hunt, 60.

The Good, the Bad, and the Ugly: Results of Adulterous Affairs

Adultery is a meanness and a stealing, a taking away from someone what should be theirs, a great selfishness, and surrounded and guarded by lies lest it should be found out. . . . And out of meanness and selfishness and lying flow love and joy and peace beyond anything that can be imagined.

Dame Rose Macaulay[1]

LOVE AFFAIRS are like wars. They are terribly exciting. But they carry a strong risk of unfathomable destruction.[2] No one can predict the outcome of an affair in advance, least of all the people involved in the affair.

The impact of a specific affair can be positive or disastrous, but seldom neutral. Many variables shape the outcome. Not uncommonly the good and the bad dimensions of an affair become so intermingled that a person feels very positively even about an adulterous relationship that has ended in ugly tragedy.

PLEASURE BEYOND MEASURE

Obviously racked by horrendous hurts, a woman sat talking with me about her past. After an extramarital affair of almost three years, her

---

1. Cited in Peter McWilliams, *Love 101: To Love Oneself Is the Beginning of a Lifelong Romance* (Los Angeles: Prelude Press, 1995), 113.
2. Richard Taylor, *Having Love Affairs* (Buffalo, NY: Prometheus Books, 1982), 188.

lover had decided he could not marry her. The man's commitment was to his job more than to his family, but the result was the same for the woman in front of me. Tears streamed down her cheeks, moistening the subtle curves of a smile shaped by her lips. Yes, a smile.

"I would do it all again," she exclaimed with a conviction defiant of her pain. "Despite the hurt I feel right now, if I had the chance, I would do it all again — with him." When I was sure my friend had fallen silent, I asked why. "How can you say that? Why would you choose a path you know would lead you into heart-rending pain?"

After moments of studied reflection, this woman described the quality of joy; the depth of communication; the sense of mutuality; and the episodes of fun, shared grief, sexual satisfaction, and spiritual identification that she had experienced with her lover. The depth and strength of the emotions with which she spoke stirred within me a feeling of "Well, of course, you would do it again. How stupid of me to ask why. You would be insane to turn down an opportunity to delve into those dimensions of life." I understood her smile, and her tears.

Obviously, that's not the whole story of an affair. Few adulterous relations fail to end without horrendous hurt, conflict, and an emotional landscape piled high with garbage-dump varieties of debris. But pleasure is a part of the story that cannot be denied — what one affair participant described as "pleasure beyond measure."

Exotic Risk

In an extramarital affair, it's difficult to distinguish between dangers and delights. Aspects of an affair that can be most destructive if other people discover the relationship contribute substantially to the durability of the affair as long as it remains a secret. Affairs thrive on secrecy and risk.

Frequently, partners in an extramarital relationship experience risk as an aphrodisiac, see secrecy as erotic, and view prohibitions as exciting incentives to venturesome actions.[3] Individuals who never really enjoyed sex in marriage suddenly find themselves sexually supercharged. Caught up in an affair, both men and women find great delight in sexual activities

3. Janet Reibstein and Martin Richards, *Sexual Arrangements: Marriage and the Temptation of Infidelity* (New York: Charles Scribner's Sons, 1993), 7; Frank S. Caprio, *Marital Infidelity* (New York: Citadel Press, 1953), 105; and Carol Botwin, *Tempted Women: The Passions, Perils, and Agonies of Female Infidelity* (New York: William Morrow, 1994), 108.

that they refused to engage in with their spouses. Anxieties produced by the affair make a lover seem more exciting than a spouse and stir emotions that feel like love.

Covert sex contributes to ecstatic pleasure for some people. Intermingled with the electric joy of "a new love" are a gleeful sense of naughtiness, the deeply satisfying pleasure of hiding something important from authority figures, and the invigoration of experimentation, ignoring barriers, and crossing new frontiers in interpersonal relations. The vehemence with which some people condemn affairs signals how "absolutely exhilarating" affairs can be.[4]

Even the risk of exposure can be a turn-on. Planning secret rendezvous takes an inordinate amount of time and requires detailed attention to logistics. Such effort brings about a preoccupation with the affair and unceasing thoughts about one's lover. All of this results in a greater commitment to the extramarital relationship. Then, as plans take shape, eagerness-laced forbidden behavior whips up a terrific surge of excitement. Mature adults exult in the thrills of adolescent sex. Trysts that cause grief also generate devotion.

The euphoria of an affair serves as an anesthetic that deadens lovers to the most serious risks of their relationship. "We thought we were invisible," a woman told me. "We acted as if other people could not see us." Such blindness sets in motion more severe risks. Life-altering consequences of sustained anxiety, guilt, insecurity, and unpredictability receive little attention. Perhaps most dangerous of all is the lovers' lack of recognition that the affair may permanently alter them personally — so dramatically changing their opinions about themselves, their views on marriage, and their feelings about their spouses that returning to their marriages vanishes as an option.[5] Neither partner in an affair can see beyond the promises of romantic spontaneity, sexual excitement, and another emotional thrill. But those are really good.

A New Kind of Love

The emotional attachment to a person that grows out of the excitement of an affair feels like love (whether it is or not) and takes its holder hostage. The affair appears totally worthwhile — worth anything and

4. Taylor, 47.
5. Reibstein and Richards, 103-4.

everything to continue — and marriage seems more and more worthless.[6]

Logic dies a quick death under the militant siege of new feelings of love. Foolishness dons the mask and mantle of wisdom. Vows of devotion proliferate — the more unrealistic, the better: "I'll do anything for you; anything, no task is too tough!" "I delight in being known as your fool." "I would be happy if we could just go somewhere together and never have to be around anybody else again." "I can live on loving you; nothing else matters." Affair partners cannot do enough to please each other, though actually it takes very little for either to experience intense pleasure as the result of some act by the other.

Does a new quality of love actually develop within an affair? Or do participants mistake lust or something else for love? Answers to those questions vary.

Here's what happens. Both people entangled in an extramarital relationship usually experience a sexual reawakening. Not uncommonly, in the early days of an affair, lovers can achieve a quality and quantity of sexual experience unparalleled in their marriages. After telling me that he had experienced four orgasms in one evening, a man declared, "I have never been capable of that in my marriage." He thought it was a sure sign of love.

As indicated above, each partner in an affair takes great pains to please the other — not just sexually. The more ridiculous one's efforts to please the other become, the more sensuous delight each derives from foolish behavior. No family baggage gets dumped onto an affair. Typically, lovers see each other apart from any identification with their parents. High-pitched romance is sustained on a daily basis apart from the disruptions of developing a fiscal budget for the relationship, paying bills, taking care of a house, assigning cleaning chores, and dealing with in-laws. A constant yearning for each other inspires lovers to make meticulous preparations for their sexual encounters. Both people stay on their best behavior in and out of bed.

No wonder the love feels new. A relationship like this cannot be maintained for long if either partner continues to live in the real world.

As the affair blurs the boundaries between fantasy and reality from the perspective of the lovers, the affair seems real and everything else

---

6. Frank S. Pittman III, *Turning Points: Treating Families in Transition and Crisis* (New York: W. W. Norton, 1987), 104.

false. As both persons romantically involved continue to fulfill their daily responsibilities in society, their affair becomes an oasis of reality in a desert of superficiality, a lifeboat of meaning in an ocean of nonmeaning.

Sooner or later, each party in an adulterous relationship tries to verify the novelty of their love by making comparisons with the offended spouses involved. These comparisons are as dangerous as they are deceptive.

In the first place, being different gets confused with being superior. Most people entering an affair choose a partner who is different from their spouse, but by no means superior to their spouse.

Second, to compare a spouse and a lover doesn't work because the comparison really turns out to be a contrast between experiences, not persons.[7] The "highs" that lovers share almost invariably stand in sharp contrast to the "plateaus" and "lows" in an intimate relationship of long duration (which also has had its "highs"). A lover's apparent superiority to a spouse resides not so much in the nature of the lover as in the difference between the conditions that surround part-time togetherness in love affairs and those that impact daily living in long-term marriages.

A powerfully appealing line of reasoning filters through the inflamed psyches of people involved in a love affair. Each lover looks at the other and thinks: "Here is a person who loves me for who I am with no ulterior reasons to do so. This individual has nothing to gain (but me) by loving me and everything to lose. I must be the lucky recipient of the greatest love imaginable." Richard Taylor concluded, "It is doubtful whether there can be found in any human experience anything as totally fulfilling as being loved in this way — intensely, intimately, and gratuitously."[8]

Growth

Occasionally an affair causes a person to get in touch with her true identity and start to live with increased emotional integrity and personal satisfaction. Why it takes an extramarital relationship to bring out such authenticity in an individual may defy explanation. It is undeniable, however, that for some people an affair becomes a context for growth.

---

7. Susan Ripps, *A Passion for More: Wives Reveal the Affairs that Make or Break Their Marriages* (New York: St. Martin's Paperbacks, 1993), xxiii.
8. Taylor, 12.

The ultimate ego-reward for a person is to see himself successfully living out a romantic role. Such an energizing vision lies at the center of an extramarital affair. As a man falls in love with his new partner, he falls in love with himself. The affair provides the occasion for the man to see himself as the person he has always wanted to be. From that perception comes a measure of self-affirmation and a level of self-confidence that change the person permanently.

In some instances an affair provides a person the first good opportunity to exhibit growth that has taken place in her life during marriage. When, for a variety of reasons, a spouse finds indications of growth threatening or offensive, a lover becomes the perfect person with whom to explore new areas of interest and demonstrate new levels of development. Buoyed by the reinforcement found in a satisfying affair, an individual often behaves in a manner that causes her spouse to say, "What's wrong with you? I hardly know who you are." All the while she is thinking to herself, "How little you really know me. This *is* who I am."

Meeting the challenges of an affair, an inflexible individual may become more flexible. A tight-lipped introvert may learn to express his feelings, even take the risk of laughing or crying with abandon. A workaholic who has always had trouble playing may learn to frolic. Hard-nosed realists sometimes find great relief in nurturing idyllic visions. A super-organized woman sometimes discovers a surprising appreciation for spontaneity.

Each of these changes in personality may indicate healthy growth. But it may also represent an unhealthy diversion. The former enhances the life of an individual, but the latter serves as a detriment.

A Discovery of Intimacy

Experts on relationships warn that a laborious determination to discover intimacy almost always backfires. The more two people work at achieving intimacy with each other, the more difficult a realization of intimacy between them becomes. Harriet Lerner observed, "Real closeness occurs most reliably not when it is pursued or demanded in a relationship, but when both individuals work consistently on their own selves."[9] Thus, an affair — a relationship initiated by two people, each of whom

9. Harriet Goldhor Lerner, *The Dance of Intimacy: A Woman's Guide to Courageous Acts of Change in Key Relationships* (New York: Harper & Row, 1989), 68.

is taking care of himself or herself—can evolve into an adventure in intimacy.

Seldom do people enter an affair conscientiously declaring a pursuit of intimacy as their purpose (even when a search for intimacy is the primary cause of the relationship). Most extramarital couples form because of a growing friendship, rampaging sexual passion, or a combination of other reasons. However, as each participant in an affair attains a measure of honesty and self-understanding individually, each also discovers something special in the relationship. Both people feel good about themselves—individually and together.

Within the emotionally charged context of an affair, two people may, for the first time in their lives, open up and discuss fears, weaknesses, and dreads as well as strengths, joys, and hopes. From the threads of personal experience, which each partner slowly unravels in the presence of the other, the couple carefully and cooperatively weaves a new fabric of relational intimacy. When this happens, regardless of the reasons the affair began, the affair continues because of its participants' delight in and enthusiastic commitment to an intimate relationship.

But What about the Marriage?

Granted that ego-affirmation, sexual gratification, new insights into the nature of love, and incentives to personal growth can be derived from an extramarital relationship, what about the marriage from which an adulterer comes? Can an affair that betrays a marriage end up contributing positively to the health of that marriage?

Many therapists insist that a person's involvement in an affair often results in a better relationship with the spouse, which in turn strengthens their marriage.[10] An affair may expose weaknesses in a marriage that when addressed therapeutically enrich that marriage. An affair can serve as a catalyst that facilitates communication between two spouses and solidifies the bond between them. Sometimes a person's pursuit of a fantasy relationship results in greater appreciation for the spouse at home.

Honestly, though, any benefits derived from an affair go almost exclusively to the spouse involved in the affair. A marriage benefits from

10. Lonnie Myers and Hunter Leggitt, *Adultery and Other Private Matters: Your Right to Personal Freedom in Marriage* (Chicago: Nelson-Hall, 1975), 104-5; Reibstein and Richards, 144-45.

an affair on the part of one of its members only if the crisis caused by the affair drives the couple into marriage therapy. Even then, improvements in the marriage typically require staggering amounts of agony and hard work by both marital partners.

Though statistics vary, estimates indicate that about 65 percent of the marriages impacted by adultery end in divorce.[11] So marital improvement based on an extramarital affair is far from a sure thing. If a marriage becomes stronger in the wake of an affair, the affair itself cannot be credited as the reason for success. Improvement in a marriage rocked by adultery depends on "the motivation of the adulterer, the self-image of the non-involved spouse . . . and the meaning the affair holds for both spouses."[12] Reasoning that an affair contributes to the health of marriage equals the flawed logic that asserts that fighting a war is the best approach to establishing peace.

HELLISH HURTS

An adulterous affair packs the wallop of an emotional hurricane. Two people involved in an extramarital relationship unleash powerful, howling, swirling blasts of emotions, which impact everybody within the couple's world (geographical, familial, and psychological). One writer described the emotions whipped to hurricane force by an affair as "virtually uncontrollable, capable of enormous destruction, unpredictable as to precisely how and where they will strike," and often marked by "moments of serene calm and beauty in between the devastating blows that are wrought."[13]

Results of an affair vary from situation to situation. However, hardly anybody in the path of the emotional rage that ensues from an affair escapes some degree of devastation. People do not discover the full magnitude of the damage inflicted by an adulterous relationship until long after the worst of the storm has subsided. Even years after the

11. Bonnie Eaker Weil, *Adultery, The Forgivable Sin* (Mamaroneck, NY: Hastings House Book Publishers, 1994), xxi.

12. Joel D. Block, *The Other Man, the Other Woman: Understanding and Coping with Extramarital Affairs* (New York: World Publishing Co., 1975), 104.

13. Frederick G. Humphrey, "Treating Sexual Relationships in Sex and Couples Therapy," *Integrating Sex and Marital Therapy: A Clinical Guide* (New York: Brunner/Mazel Publishers, 1987), 149.

turbulence, individuals keep finding and clearing away debris left over from the event.

Marital Conflict

Most marriage and family therapists pull no punches in describing the tragic consequences of an extramarital affair. Fogarty asserted, "Adultery has a devastating impact on the entire family system."[14] Focusing on marital partners affected by adultery, Weil declared, "Adultery destroys any relationship it touches."[15]

Betraying Love

On several occasions, I have seen individuals only minutes after discovering they have been betrayed by an adulterous spouse. No other agony approaches their condition. Whether by excruciating wails or deafening silence, betrayed spouses appear to have taken a heavy blow to the gut. More than once I have heard one of these individuals remark, "It would be easier if I had discovered he was dead."

Within a marriage that has been marked by trust, the revelation of an adulterous affair shatters a betrayed spouse like nothing else.[16] Reactions run the gamut of emotions. From initial hurt comes horrible anger. Shock gives way to serious plans for retaliation. Disbelief recedes in the face of an obsession to find out the details of what happened. Episodes of weeping and outbursts of near hatred defy appropriate circumstances.

"But we made promises to each other!" a woman shouts at her unfaithful husband. "Does your word mean nothing any more? How can I ever trust you again?" Similarly, between heaves and sobs, a man speaks to his adulterous wife: "I never questioned your love; not for one minute. I thought we were all right, secure. I really believed you loved me. How could I be so wrong?" There's the issue — a betrayal of love. A betrayal of love causes hurt of unparalleled proportions. Such infidelity throws into question a couple's past as well as their present and future.

Once the weeping stops, waves of hurt recede a bit, and anger stills,

14. Weil, xi.
15. Weil, xxi.
16. Carol Botwin, *Men Who Can't Be Faithful* (New York: Warner Books, 1988), 156-57.

a betrayed spouse may begin a devastating process of self-blame. Wanting to believe his marital partner is really as faithful as he thought, a husband reasons, "I let her down; I didn't give her what she needed." A wife berates herself, "I stopped worrying about my looks; I've become unattractive; I'm unappealing." After discovering a spouse's involvement in an extramarital affair, many marriage partners go through dramatic weight loss, concerted attention to attractive clothing, and hyperintensive efforts to be pleasing.

Betrayal hurts both the betrayed and the adulterer. A loss of trust devastates each one. Questions about the renewal of trust hover over their relationship like a dark, threatening cloud.

A majority of marital partners hurt by adultery end up in a divorce court. Betrayals of love tend to rip the heart out of even very strong relationships.

Hurting the Innocent

Drop a big rock in the middle of a pond and you'll get an idea of the influence of an adulterous relationship. An affair sends ripple after ripple of trouble washing across each family unit involved and lapping at the extremities of the participants' community.

Children live close to the center of the turbulence. They bear much more of the brunt of an affair than they should. At home, they sense tension, if not experience conflict. In public, they feel embarrassment, if not receive harassment. Worse still, children of people in an affair see their security threatened and the stability of their futures destroyed. Sadly, some children feel they must side with one parent against the other in moments of conflict. Others try to referee arguments between their parents and to bring about reconciliation. Occasionally, children assume that they are the cause of adultery-related conflict in their home.

Watching innocent children suffer as a result of their illicit behavior causes affair partners to deromanticize an idyllic relationship and to second-guess their actions. Prolonged suffering in these children's lives — whether because of a public spectacle, a financial shortage resulting from the loss of a job, a divorce, or a move — inflicts long-lasting guilt on their adulterous parents.

When affair partners who are parents end up marrying each other, the children involved often develop deep resentment. Each child looks askance at the person who caused her parent to leave home. Likewise, a child resents anyone other than a family member making his parent extremely happy. Integrating children into second marriages proves difficult even in the best of situations.

Other family members, friends, and colleagues at work feel the ripple effect of an affair as they shoulder hardships that wash over them. Parents, aunts, and uncles pitch in to care for the offended spouse and confused children or to stand by the adulterer. Sometimes they have to supply financial assistance. Friends grow tense over conflicting loyalties and reluctantly choose to lend their support to only one partner in a marriage. An entire business can be disrupted by an affair that develops in the workplace.

None of these people deserve to suffer because of an affair. But an affair is not about fairness.

Fearing Reprisals

Once exposed as adulterers, persons become almost paranoid about reprisals. "Who is going to take a shot at me next?" a man cynically asks. "When is another shoe going to drop?" a distraught woman wonders aloud. Adulterers worry about how knowledge of their behavior will affect their jobs; influence the treatment they receive from friends, colleagues, and clients; and alter their status within a religious fellowship.

Grave anxieties arise from trying to anticipate a spouse's reactions to infidelity. "You know something is coming," one weary husband complained. "You just don't know what's next." Offended wives and offended husbands do not react to an adulterous spouse in the same manner.

Generally speaking, males respond to a spouse's betrayal with less show of emotions than females. A betrayed husband may give his guilty wife the silent treatment — "Let her stew in her own stuff." Or he may punish her by withholding money she needs or sexual experiences she desires — "Why should I have sex with you? You'll just compare me to your lover!" Threats of violence incite panic — "Do you want me to kill you or your lover, or both of you?" A husband may leave home for a while — "I've got to have some time away from you; every time I look at you it hurts." Not uncommonly an offended husband gets back at his adulterous wife through an addiction that can spell ruin for him and her — "Why shouldn't I roll the dice for fun and profit? At least I don't screw around like you."

Betrayal by a husband tends to shove wives through a wide span of emotional responses. Initially, a hurting woman may appeal to her spouse's sympathy, especially if she knows he already feels guilty over his infidelity. Tears flow freely as she frequently complains of her discomfort. However, sentimentality often escalates into volatility. Offended wives may throw wild temper tantrums and physically strike their husbands. Occasionally a distraught wife goes on a shopping spree with the intention of inflicting financial difficulties on her spouse. More passively, wives retaliate for their husbands' adultery by refusing to perform household chores that they always have done, serving cold meals, and ignoring their spouses' normal emotional and sexual needs.

Occasionally, when rocked by a spouse's affair, the offended spouse initiates an affair. No love is involved, only an angry payback. But anger can generate great passion even if emptiness follows.

Of course, divorce is never out of the question after the revelation of an affair. Seldom does any marriage rocked by adulterous behavior escape serious talk of separation and divorce. Well over half the time, marital partners troubled by adultery terminate their relationship. Statistically, divorce following adultery is more common when the wife has been the guilty spouse.

Fearing reprisals goes with the territory for a person adjusting to life as an exposed adulterer. Husbands and wives respond to unfaithful spouses differently, but both find ways to begin to get even.

Struggling with Truth

Counselors vigorously debate whether or not an affair that has been terminated prior to discovery should be disclosed to one's marital partner. For therapists, the issue is somewhat hypothetical. Not so for adulterers. Questions about confession stir up a terrific struggle within an affair participant's soul.

Plenty of "good" reasons exist for not telling a spouse about an extramarital affair. "It's over," a weary husband argues, "and I'm back in the marriage with every intention of staying. A confession of my infidelity will just make it more difficult for the marriage to survive, and I want it to survive." "What he doesn't know about me can't hurt him," a participant in two affairs told me, "but it sure could hurt me. What if my husband should explode in anger and try to take my children away from me? I won't risk that happening." At least the reasons for silence sound "good" to the people keeping secrets. But seldom can they see the whole relational picture.

Long-time counselor Frank Pittman adamantly insists that adulterers confess infidelity to their spouses. Always. A refusal to be honest represents a barrier to intimacy. According to Pittman, "The lie may be a greater betrayal of the relationship than the misdeed being lied about."[17] Ultimately, dishonesty harms a marriage more than sexual infidelity. In Pittman's words, "It isn't whom you lie with. It's whom you lie to."[18]

Not all therapists agree with Pittman. One clinical professor of psychology argues that, in most cases, undiscovered infidelity should not be confessed. This professional sees a confession of infidelity as a source of relief for the adulterer and a source of harm for the betrayed spouse, thus a selfish act.[19] Some proponents of this view not only advise against telling about adultery but recommend lying about adultery, if necessary, for the good of the offended marital partner.

Internal battles over whether or not to confess an affair to a spouse take on the feel of a life-or-death struggle. A confession of infidelity probably will set off a dangerous display of emotional fireworks immediately. Over the long haul, though, talking about an affair with one's spouse creates the possibility of renewed, maybe even increased, intimacy within the marriage. Knowing that, however, makes neither the decision to tell nor the telling any easier.

Social Judgment

Social attitudes are fickle. A society fascinated by adultery reacts harshly to adulterers. The same persons who pay big bucks for entertainment based on illicit affairs look with disdain on friends and neighbors caught in extramarital relationships. One adulterous man declared in a disappointment-riddled voice, "You can't count on anybody, not even your friends, when this happens."

In the midst of an affair, lovers usually discuss persons who they think can be counted on to stand by them in a time of need. Blinded to

17. Frank Pittman, *Private Lies: Infidelity and the Betrayal of Intimacy* (New York: W. W. Norton, 1989), 59.

18. Pittman, *Private Lies,* 53.

19. Block, 75. Kinder and Cowan agree, asserting that people who confess "only wish . . . to relieve themselves of the horrible secret and expiate their guilt" and predicting that a confession may do irreparable harm. Melvyn Kinder and Connell Cowan, *Husbands and Wives: Exploring Marital Myths, Deepening Love and Desire* (New York: Clarkson N. Potter, 1989), 100.

reality by a romantic fog, they name almost everybody they know. Once under siege because of their adulterous behavior, affair participants invariably see their list of anticipated supporters dwindle rapidly. "Virtually everybody" becomes "almost nobody." Worse still, in the wake of an affair, an anticipated supporter often becomes an inflicter of hurt.

Ugly Gossip

Social gatherings thrive on gossip. The topic of a suspected or revealed affair has no equals in terms of interest. "Can you believe it?" the whispers begin. "Have you heard?" a person not wanting to appear the last to know asks a new arrival. The excitement of an inappropriate conversation stirs erotic interests and blunts all sensitivity to the feelings of the persons being discussed.

A lack of accurate information is of little consequence in circles of social gossip. Self-acclaimed authorities level libelous charges, pass vicious judgments, and offer biting criticisms apart from any real knowledge of the situation of the people whom they castigate. Public talk worsens the problem for everybody related to an adulterous relationship, even if the rhetoric is accurate. Both participants and their innocent family members suffer from their unsought status as public spectacles.

Loss of Respect

Few if any other acts of wrongdoing carry the social stigma of adultery. Society assigns the deadly label of "a morals charge" exclusively to persons guilty of sexual infidelity or other sexual misdeeds (as if no other sin merits so destructive a tag).

Talk may be cheap, but a loss of respect is expensive. When people see to it that adultery dominates a person's reputation, jobs are lost, careers scuttled, and families hurt. Sometimes a social group completely destroys an adulterer's future. What's worse, the people involved feel good about what they have done. "He had it coming to him," a member of one such group explained.

Ostracism

Unfortunately, at the very moment when a person reeling under the fallout of an adulterous relationship needs fellowship as never before, most folks turn away. Fearing support for the person may be misunderstood as support for the person's behavior, many people withhold even so much as a kind telephone call to a former friend exposed as an adulterer.

Recently, in my presence, two women compared notes about the treatment they received from churches in which they were members. Both were made to feel unwelcome. A minister in one of the congregations told his parishioner pointedly, "We had rather you not come just now; you make us uncomfortable. We're not sure how to relate to you." Now get this: the only fault to be found in these hurting women was that both were married to men who had recently been involved in an extramarital affair.

Even a permissive, promiscuous society responds to revelations of adultery with moral snobbery. And it hurts; it hurts badly.

Personal Pain

Bed hoppers rarely recognize the danger of their lifestyle or focus on the potential hurts with which they flirt. Each new sexual climax seems to more than compensate for any anxiety about potential problems. Eventually, though, the costs of an adulterous hobby have to be paid. And, unfortunately, pain rather than money is the only currency that counts.

The more deeply involved in an affair a person becomes, the more difficulty that person has thinking clearly about anything. A thick fog covers life like a pall. Disorientation and confusion prevail. A man can hardly see, much less understand, what is going on right under his nose. Sorting out sources of pain and isolating problems related to the affair are virtually impossible tasks. At one moment a person in an affair feels great, on top of the world, and the next moment he feels terrible, like the weight of the world is on his back.

Problems and hurts that arise in the normal course of an affair multiply as well as intensify once an affair ends, regardless of how it ends. A quiet agreement to terminate a long-lasting adulterous relationship spawns heart-breaking pain for the lovers involved. So does a decision by adulterous lovers to end their marriages, though the twists and turns of these hurts differ considerably from those involved in ending the affair. When an affair comes to a screeching halt because a betrayed spouse or an irate employer discovers the illicit relationship, watch out. A firestorm of anger, pain, hurt, hatred, accusations, resentment, and threats is certain to sweep across the landscape.

Fatigue

Extramarital affairs take work. Even relationships that begin spontaneously ("It just happened!") endure only with considerable effort.

Every contact between lovers requires careful planning in advance and detailed deception afterward. Meticulous thought must be devoted to where lovers will meet, how they will get there, and what time of the day is safest. Schedules have to be adjusted to provide free time that can be reported later as a busy time, should anyone inquire. Work assignments left undone because of a rendezvous must be covered in a manner that doesn't precipitate questions or raise suspicions. Affair participants have to devise explanations for money spent on the affair that will be acceptable within their families. One slipup and everybody is in trouble.

Just keeping in touch with each other is no easy task for two people engaged in an adulterous relationship. Who can call when? Each needs to keep in mind the schedule of the other's household and workplace. Is it safe to call the office? Is one time better than another? When are you alone? How many times a day dare we call each other? Weekends and holidays present special problems because all schedules change. Efforts to keep in touch can exact a heavy toll of physical and emotional energy from the lovers involved.

Add to these worries about planning and calling each other a relentless anxiety about secrecy and the practice of deception. Does anyone suspect us? Can our friends look at us and tell something is going on? Lying is not easy, especially lies that rest on the believability of other lies. What did I tell her last time? Does he realize that my facts don't match? Deception ravages energy. Nothing takes more effort than trying to cover real feelings with superficial words and contradictory actions.

When a person in an affair becomes obsessed with the possibility of discovery, fatigue worsens. Worried lovers confess not being able to sleep at night for fear of speaking their partner's name aloud while dreaming. Others become fearful every time a telephone or a doorbell rings. Paranoia about secrecy destroys an ability to rest. Fatigue worsens.

At some point in an extended affair, fatigue borders on, if not develops into, exhaustion. A person becomes so tired of protecting an illicit relationship that she carelessly (though sometimes it can be intentionally) creates the likelihood of being discovered. Exposure will bring hurt, but also relief and maybe rest.

Guilt

Sometimes guilt arises on day one of an adulterous relationship. In other instances, guilt shows up only after a lengthy period of delay. Regardless of the schedule on which guilt arrives (as it almost invariably does), the emergence of guilt in a person signals the beginning of a long and painful struggle.

Not all guilt is bad. Just as physical pain signals a physiological problem in need of attention, guilt raises proper questions about the behavior causing it. That's good. Identifying a source of pain makes it possible for a biological disorder to be cured. Likewise, guilt can inspire corrective actions related to its causes. Legitimate guilt serves a redemptive purpose.

Problems arise when a person bears guilt apart from efforts to acknowledge it honestly and alleviate it. Knowing the source of guilt and despising the presence of guilt while continuing the behavior that causes the guilt is a deadly mix. Caught in this vicious cycle, a person grows increasingly guilty and increasingly angry — guilty because of what he is doing and angry because he can't stop doing it. Ultimately, unrelieved guilt robs a person of self-confidence and destroys any hope of lifestyle changes that will improve his lot.

Continued guilt festers like a sore, sending infection and inflammation coursing throughout a person's emotional-spiritual system. Sickness follows — not imagined sickness, real illness. Symptoms may include an ulcer, bad headaches, depression, severe fluctuations in weight, and listlessness, but the real problem is un-dealt-with guilt.

Affairs abound with opportunities (and legitimate reasons) for guilt. A participant may feel guilt over breaking her marriage vows, risking hurt for her children, violating her morality of sex, disappointing friends, jeopardizing a career, and perpetuating dishonesty. Guilt can arise in relation to an affair partner as well: "I fear I have taken advantage of her." "Knowing I can't marry him, I should not allow this to continue." "I can't love her like I want to because of so many distractions." "I am jeopardizing his life as well as mine."

Acts of love within an affair participant's family make matters worse. The lighthearted joy of his children or a thoughtful gesture by his wife intensifies the already heavy guilt carried by an individual involved in an extramarital relationship. A spouse's simple "I love you" feels like a slap in the face.

A confession of guilt is a prerequisite for therapeutic punishment or cleansing from guilt. Individuals who refuse to acknowledge their guilt often embark on a course of self-punishment; it seems like the "reasonable" thing to do — "If I'm not going to receive the punishment I rightly have coming to me from others, I will punish myself." Seldom is this a conscious act. Even their guilt may be unconscious. Nevertheless, destructive results ensue.

An unfaithful husband may become sexually dysfunctional in relation to his wife (whether or not she knows of his infidelity). No physiological problem exists, only the man's subconscious refusal to permit himself to enjoy sexual pleasure. Likewise, an unfaithful wife may permit an unwanted pregnancy with her husband to "atone" for her sins and end an affair.

Most marriage therapists agree that men handle guilt better than women.[20] Typically, a man segments his life and emotions in a manner almost impossible for a woman to achieve. Also, women usually feel more guilt about extramarital sex than men because they set infidelity in a larger social context and more readily view its consequences for others. However, neither men nor women do well with guilt over an extended period of time. Nobody does.

Anger

Anger seethes just beneath the surface in most affairs. Given half a chance for expression, anger explodes into visibility with life-threatening force.

Sources of anger vary considerably. At some point, affair participants usually get angry at their spouses — "Here we are, in a relationship of boundless happiness, prevented from being together because of two people (spouses) who have never made us happy and wouldn't know happiness if it hit them in the face." An enraged sense of unfairness can lead to hypothetical discussions of their spouses' deaths. Not uncommonly, such anger proceeds to violence. Less frequently, but occasionally, this anger results in murder.

Anger can be turned inward — "How did I let myself get in this situation? Yes, I love my partner, but I am jeopardizing everything else in my life. I see no good way out. What an idiot I am!" Acknowledged and channeled responsibly, self-directed anger can benefit the realization of needed changes. Repressed and left to intensify, though, such anger breeds depression or worse.

When an affair ends because of an independent decision by one of the participants, blasts of anger broadside the relationship — "You traitor! How could you draw me deeper and deeper into this relationship over all these months and then go back to your spouse? What about the

---

20. Reibstein and Richards, 98, 141-42.

promises you made to me, what about the love you professed, what about our plans and dreams?" Angry threats often follow: "I will tell your husband everything. You can't treat me like this and get away with it. I will see to it that he won't take you back."

When confronted and charged with wrongdoing by their spouses, adulterers often turn their anger toward these betrayed persons — "Yes, I have done wrong, but you made me do it. You have never understood me and obviously still don't. Why can't you see how you're wrong?"

Of course, the anger of an offended spouse after the revelation of an affair can be taken for granted — "You lousy Judas! How could you do this to your children and to me? Right now I don't want to hear your mealymouthed explanations. Go talk to your whore. Get the hell out of my sight!"

Affairs are to anger what a hydroelectric plant is to energy. Count on it.

Memories

Memories can soothe emotions or incite them. In the aftermath of an affair, memories seem to do both at the same time.

The end of an affair launches a fleet of memories that may not ever sail completely out of the reach of two people once involved with each other. A specific remnant from the past that returns to memory like a blessing may at another time come back as a curse. Amid an affair participant's longing for her separated lover, she cherishes images of past intimacies. Let those same pictures from the past interrupt her concentration on reconciliation in a crucial conversation with her spouse, however, and the memories explode like bombs, disrupting everything and filling the air with emotional shrapnel.

Memory fails to provide a consistent, accurate re-creation of the past. When hurt or anger dominates an individual's feelings about a former lover, his memory tends to reinforce those emotions by blocking out positive dimensions of the relationship and presenting only its negative aspects. Conversely, nostalgia for the past often ignores all but the best moments in an affair. Both situations present problems. Inaccurate recalls of the past hinder honest attempts to deal with the present and block efforts to get on with the future.

Affairs that end indecisively or prior to physical intimacy — whether because of discovery by a spouse, a warning at the office, a geographical move, or some other reason — spawn the most unmanageable memories. Forced termination of a relationship between two lovers interrupts their plans, dreams, and hopes. Devoid of an opportunity to discover for themselves the difficulties involved in a pursuit of their plans, lovers may idealize the whole relationship — "It could have been perfect," they tell themselves. "This could have been the best relationship ever." Idyllic memories of an affair cripple the resolve required to recommit to a marriage. Disrupted lovers cling to romantic expectations that can never be matched as they look back to a relationship larger than life.

Emotional Illness

Emotional trauma may contribute to the beginning of an affair. At the conclusion of an affair, emotional illness is always a possibility. Not everyone who exits an adulterous relationship succumbs to emotional difficulties, but many do.

An affair exacts a heavy toll from any participant with minimal sensitivity. Desires conflict with obligations, religious convictions clash with personal wishes, fulfillment battles guilt, and honesty struggles with deception. An emotional civil war rages internally. And like any war, this conflict produces casualties.

When a meaningful affair ends in secrecy, participants avoid trauma-producers associated with public exposure. However, the two hurting people are deprived of badly needed sympathy and emotional support from others. Their yearnings continue. A sense of loss prevails. The grief process begins. Anger and resentment threaten to erupt. Yet each of the pained persons tries to repress emotions that, should they find expression, would raise major questions in the minds of significant other people.

When an affair ends in public, participants can express their emotions more freely, but their emotions must withstand an even heavier assault. In addition to dealing with profound personal hurts, adulterous partners have to face barrages of anger from their spouses, heart-wrenching displays of disappointment from their children, threatening interrogations from their friends, condemnation from judgmental acquaintances, and anxieties prompted by criticisms from professional colleagues. Taken altogether, it's more than some people can stand.

Not uncommonly, emotional illness accompanies a person's exit from an extramarital affair. Even if the individual succeeded in hiding the affair, the illness produced by the extramarital relationship defies secrecy. Some people can't stop weeping. Others allow humiliation to pummel them into a near-catatonic state of isolation. Clinical depression may develop. Often jealousy escalates into a furious rage. Not infrequently an addiction develops — drinking, gambling, shopping, or working.

Occasionally, in the aftermath of an affair, emotional dis-ease escalates to an extreme point of danger. Violence ensues. The rationale of a sick love justifies inflicting physical harm on a former lover. Or, in a twisted mental state fed by feelings of failure, remorse, anger, and revenge, a person takes his own life.

An adulterous affair has the power to make a person extremely happy and deathly ill. One perceptive student of adulterous relations concluded, "Only a small percentage of men and women in our society have fully freed themselves of deep-seated anxieties and guilts about extramarital relations."[21]

Reputation

A woman finished reminiscing aloud about her involvement in a series of extramarital affairs. She quipped defensively, "I really don't care what anyone else thinks about me. My affairs are nobody's business but my own."

Noticeably badly shaken, a respected church and community leader stammered and stuttered through a confession of his long-term involvement in an adulterous relationship. Bowing his head, the man mumbled almost inaudibly, "I knew from the first moment that my reputation would never be the same again. Even if nobody else had ever found out, I knew what had happened, what I had done. But now others know."

What strikingly different attitudes these two people possessed, at least on the surface. Few are the people who honestly don't care about their reputation.

The revelation of an adulterous affair is like the opening of hunting season (free game!). It seems to offer a general invitation for public criticism. An individual holding public office or occupying a highly visible position in a community can count on the media's exposure of her infidelity. An employee of a church or another religious organization can anticipate immediate termination professionally as well as strident

21. Block, 21.

criticism individually. Other individuals guilty of adultery may not suffer from such broad-based public discussions of their private behavior, but they surely will serve as popular subjects for lively conversations at civic club gatherings, over drinks in a local restaurant, and after the benediction at a Bible study group.

When a person charged with adultery walks into a room, she feels like everybody present turns to look at her as a prelude to whispering about her sin. "My face burned," one woman in this situation complained. Another deeply troubled woman, exuding bitter resentment and anger, told me, "My reputation is shot. I can't even attend a worship service in my church without people treating me like I have a disease." In a long-distance telephone call, a friend two years past an extramarital relationship pleaded for help: "Can you say a good word for me? My former supervisor scuttles every employment opportunity I have by warning people that I have a bad reputation."

Tragically, in the minds of many people, an act of adultery becomes a source of identity for the persons involved. "Oh, you know him," someone whispers in a public gathering. "He is the man who had an affair with the woman who worked in that restaurant downtown." A reputation as an adulterer may last a lifetime.

For certain individuals, a bad reputation doesn't seem to matter. Nevertheless, most folks grow weary of wearing an "adulterer" tag and carrying the baggage of infidelity. Despite the benefit of "thick skin" insensitive to painful public criticism, a bad reputation can cause an adulterer major problems — severely limiting her earning power and restricting promotions professionally, or even preventing certain types of employment.

So potent is adultery's power to ruin a person's reputation that charges of adultery do not even have to be true to hurt a person badly. A hint of an affair or the appearance of a indiscreet relationship often accomplishes the kind of character assassination associated with the reality of an extramarital relationship.

TRYING TO GET ON WITH LIFE

A person who has been involved in an adulterous relationship never completely gets over it. If the affair in any way emulated a marriage, problems with moving beyond it intensify.

Discomfort

Uncomfortable situations arise at unexpected times and catch adulterers off guard. A woman watching television with family members suddenly grows fidgety as a dramatized story about an adulterous wife begins. "What are they thinking?" she wonders to herself. "Will someone ask me about my affair?" Guilt or remorse or both stir discomfort. Similarly, a man driving to work feels his heart skip a beat as a certain song comes over the car radio. This was a piece of music of special importance in his love affair of long ago. "I have not thought of her for quite a while," he muses. "I can't believe I still miss her." Nostalgia and regrets feed discomfort.

Despite good intentions to allow the matter to drop, once-betrayed spouses periodically resurface the adultery issue in their marriages. In the middle of an argument, a husband hurls a reference to her former adultery at his spouse, hoping to hurt her. A wife questions her husband about a past affair because of lingering inquisitiveness and nervousness. Regardless of the time and reason for opening up the painful subject again, the result almost always includes anger, hurt, and distancing. Continuing to revisit a prior relationship brings more discomfort to the present and raises questions about the future.

Occasionally, former affair partners act to assure that life does not continue normally for their once-upon-a-time lovers. "I'm gonna give him a taste of what I'm still going through. It ain't all hunky-dory for me," a woman bitterly commented.

Recently, I have watched previous partners in two long-term affairs broadside their former lovers, who happily moved back into their marriages to lead productive lives. Each achieved the intention — major disruption. As a result of the vindictive efforts of a lover from nearly a decade ago, one man lost his job. The other individual has guaranteed that his former love will live daily with deep-seated fears and nagging regrets.

Promise and Hope

Involvement in an affair does not have to end in total disaster. An individual can live beyond an adulterous relationship (or relationships). A marriage can survive infidelity by one or both partners. Immediate consequences of an affair are almost always hellish in nature. But an affair, like other emotional experiences, can cause an individual to deal with major problems therapeutically, move toward maturity, and learn the joy of commitment in a marital relationship.

Mistaken religious concepts about sin, adultery, forgiveness, and grace stand in the way of growth and promise as well as destroy hope for many adulterers. These same misperceptions cause other people (often well meaning) to block adulterers' best efforts to get on with life. A lack of understanding about basic biblical truths reinforces these detrimental ideas and assures defeating actions.

If adultery is an unforgivable sin, for example, then one act of infidelity ruins life forever. But is adultery unforgivable? Does an extramarital affair belong in a special moral category, destined for treatment like that directed toward no other act of wrongdoing? What does the Bible teach about adultery and the promise of life after adultery? To these questions we turn our attention on the following pages.

PART II

AN UNPARDONABLE SIN?

Hester and Arthur

Adultery is such an overratedly fascinating sin.

Robert Farrar Capon[1]

WHEN HESTER Prynne committed adultery, her neighbors responded with mean retribution. Members of Hester's church displayed attitudes and actions toward her every bit as wrong as the sin that they condemned.

What a familiar story. In this instance, the account is fictional. Nathaniel Hawthorne penned the classic narrative about Hester Prynne known as *The Scarlet Letter*. Change the names, dates, and scenery, though, and you have a sad commentary on many contemporary situations, attitudes, and actions.

The pious Puritans of early Boston made virtually no distinction between law and morality (the scaffold used by the community in its treatment of criminals stood almost squarely beneath the eves of Boston's earliest church). These legalists of the first order considered adultery a sin like no other. Thus, when they discovered Hester Prynne's adulterous guilt, they treated her wrongdoing as a civil offense. Subsequently, decisions about a proper punishment for Hester's hideous act fell to the local magistrates.

Boston's agents of justice ruled that Hester Prynne must stand on the platform of the pillory for a period of three hours — a picture of

---

1. Robert Farrar Capon, *Health, Money, and Love . . . and Why We Don't Enjoy Them* (Grand Rapids: Eerdmans, 1990), 111.

71

unspeakable shame, a public spectacle of moral failure. Additionally, officials instructed Hester never again to appear in public without displaying on the breast of her gown a scarlet letter — a letter that symbolically announced the nature of her sin, warned others of the terrible consequences of an adulterous act, and served as a form of "endless retribution."[2]

Only "church members in good repute" objected to the magistrates' sentence for Hester the sinner.[3] They considered the prescribed punishment too merciful. One "autumnal matron" called for "the brand of a hot iron" to be placed on Hester's forehead.[4] Another shouted that the shame engendered by Hester's act justified taking her life. These starchy enemies of iniquity argued that no form of punishment could be too severe for a woman who committed adultery in "our godly New England."[5] What's more, they based their incensed vindictiveness on the teachings of the Bible — "Is there not law for it? Truly there is, both in the Scripture and the statue-book."[6]

When Hester Prynne appeared in public, she wore on her clothes the letter *A* — *A* for adultery, *A* for adulteress. Thereby, every time she ventured into the community, Hester placarded a reminder of the shame, banishment, and solitude that must be borne by anyone who committed adultery. As bad as that was, attendance in a meeting of the church was worse. When Hester showed up for worship, she became the subject of the sermon.

In his chilling tale of Hester Prynne, Nathaniel Hawthorne painted an accurate picture of the strength (and meanness) of self-righteousness among much of the citizenry in colonial America. Good people understood godliness more in terms of harsh judgments against sin than of extensions of mercy to sinners. By decreeing that Hester Prynne forever wear a scarlet letter, the saints of Boston declared that this woman should always be defined by her sin. They tolerated no distinction between a person and a person's action. Regardless of the nature of Hester's future, she could never live beyond an immoral act in her past — because that immoral act was adultery.

2. Nathaniel Hawthorne, *The Scarlet Letter* (New York: New American Library, 1959), 84.

3. Hawthorne, 59.

4. Hawthorne, 59.

5. Hawthorne, 68.

6. Hawthorne, 59.

Many people today read Nathaniel Hawthorne's stirring tale of Hester Prynne and recoil in protest. How ludicrous, prudish, and just plain wrong. But wait. Adultery remains a special sin in the minds of innumerable folks and still an illegal form of behavior — a criminal act — in some states. Plenty of people continue to insist that individuals guilty of adultery receive a punishment of extreme severity, which guarantees a relentless charge of shame. And, as in Hawthorne's Boston of old, often the most vocal agents of mean-spirited retribution claim membership in a church and spit out their poisonous platitudes in the name of God.

Is Hawthorne's classic narrative a relic from the past or a mirror of powerful and pervasive attitudes extant in the present?

Today, not even the most pious people among us call for the physical death of an adulterous person. Scores of people, however, stand ready to take aim and fire round after round of ammunition to inflict social, professional, and spiritual death on adulterers. Some individuals thrive on preparing scarlet letters, hunting down those who (in their opinions) deserve to wear them, and attaching their handmade badges of disgrace to the visible fabric of people's characters. Self-appointed defenders of righteousness want all who "fall short" to be seen and known as moral failures. The alarming words with which Nathaniel Hawthorne concluded his tragic account of Hester Prynne ring with reality: "Let not the reader argue . . . that the times of the Puritans were more vicious than our own."[7]

What's the deal here? Why this fascination with "the scarlet letter"? Why this unique hangup with adultery? What is the source of people's graceless reactions to adulterers — culture or Scripture? And why do the most severe judgments about adulterers and the most hurtful reactions to adulterers almost invariably come from individuals who should know better than anyone else the pervasiveness of sin among humankind and the all-sufficient thoroughness of divine forgiveness? Does denouncing people who fail morally and working to assure that they can never outlive their sins in some strange way strengthen morality? What is the role of the gospel of redemption in shaping Christians' reactions to persons guilty of the sin of adultery? Or does adultery lie beyond the realm of redemption, thus leaving adulterers to fend for themselves devoid of the promises of the gospel?

7. Hawthorne, 249.

Ironically, the harshest critics of adulterers usually employ a medley of Scripture verses to justify their criticism. In a spirit akin to that of the marauding Crusaders, resolute in their efforts to wipe out heresy, insensitive individuals use the Bible as a spear with which to stab adulterers rather than as a revelation from God with which to offer them forgiveness and hope. Getting rid of adulterers seems more holy than embracing them with grace. As a result, persons massaging the emotional aches acquired in an adulterous relationship quickly turn away from the Christian community, fearing more hurt and feeling that they have hurt enough already. Christians breathe a sigh of relief and whisper, "Good riddance."

When adultery causes separation between a person and a Christian community, both moral crusaders and immoral adulterers give credibility to a damnable biblical heresy. They allow adultery to become the defining event in a person's life. They consent to adultery standing as a barrier beyond which an adulterer cannot go and through which the gospel cannot penetrate. Such an attitude constitutes far greater immorality than does the sin to which it is directed.

What the Bible says about adultery is important, very important. Equally significant, though, is what the Bible says about the nature of God, the message of the gospel, the primacy of grace, and the mission of the people of God in relation to persons who have committed adultery. Adulterers do not stand outside the reach of the good news of the gospel, an exception to the promise of redemption. Adultery is not an unpardonable sin.

Consider carefully the Bible's teachings about adultery and grace.

Law Has No Answer

If . . . you should encounter Saint Peter, ask him to rescind [the commandments], as they are . . . too hindersome for good Christians.

Benjamin Franklin
(after confessing to the sin of adultery)[1]

IS ADULTERY an (or *the*) unpardonable sin? Unfortunately, responding honestly to this inquiry is not all that simple; and I place a premium on honesty. Only truth offers any help to people interested in living with integrity.

If you like neat, succinct answers to all questions, you probably won't care much for the discussion that follows. Personally, I don't prefer complexity to simplicity. However, to ignore or to minimize obvious, unmistakable complexity in order to serve the cause of simplicity is as wrong as seeking to make a plain, simple truth obtuse and difficult to understand. Both acts qualify as dishonesty, a hindrance rather than a contributor to authentic morality. Only an awareness of the complexity of moral decision making and ethical (or unethical) actions can prevent judgmental decrees that are simple to a fault.

An honest response to the moral severity of adultery requires defining adultery, the scope of forgiveness, and the nature of God's grace.

---

1. Benjamin Franklin, *Dr. Benjamin Franklin and the Ladies* (Mt. Vernon, NY: Peter Pauper, 1939), 34, cited in Philip E. Lampe, "Adultery and the Twenty-First Century," *Adultery in the United States: Close Encounters of the Sixth (or Seventh) Kind* (Buffalo, NY: Prometheus Books, 1987), 203-4.

Only by means of carefully spelled-out definitions can conversationalists be sure they are talking about the same thing. Then, too, attention must be devoted to the teachings of the Bible. Most people who position adultery as a unique sin standing beyond the scope of normal forgiveness claim the Bible as the basis of their opinion. Have they read the Scriptures correctly? What does the Bible say — both explicitly and implicitly — about adultery?

ELUSIVE DEFINITIONS

Legalism helps very little, if at all, in establishing the kind of helpful definitions that inform good judgments about the morality of certain actions. A typical legalist displays a passion for simplicity — an act is either right or wrong. "It's as simple as that." However, when specific cases of personal behavior fail to fit into one of several legal categories (or codes), legalists don't know what to do. Maybe that's just as well.

The difficulty of defining behavior theologically and morally highlights the danger of making smug evaluations about an individual's actions and issuing pronouncements regarding the nature of a person's character. Though all of us seem prone to flirt with that danger from time to time, resisting such a tendency qualifies as practically smart and spiritually sound. Finite individuals — even those who know every last word of the law — cannot accurately pass judgments on the moral makeup of each other.

Marriage: Spiritual Covenant or Legal Contract

During the reception that followed the marriage ceremony for my wife and me, one of my uncles raced up to us to declare excitedly, "You're not really married." "Why?" I immediately wanted to know. "Because," he said, "the minister didn't say 'What God hath joined together, let not man put asunder.'" In my uncle's mind, the legitimacy of a marriage hinged on the reenactment of a particular ceremony containing a verbatim recitation of specific words.

My genuinely concerned relative was not the first to question when marriage occurs. Neither was his answer to that query an isolated attempt to provide a legalistic definition of marriage.

Questions about marriage abound: Does a relationship become a marriage only when both members of a couple state their promises of fidelity to each other? Do these vows of love and faithfulness become valid only when someone else hears them? Must a representative of the government acknowledge a couple's promises to assure a marriage? Is the pronouncement of the one presiding at a wedding — "I now pronounce you husband and wife" — a prerequisite to the making of a marriage? Or does marriage occur at the moment of the first experience of sexual intercourse between two people? Maybe the most fundamental question about marriage presses the issue of whether marriage is a civil, spiritual, or physical phenomenon, or a blend of all these.

Finding biblical answers to these crucial questions is not as easy as one might think. The Bible spans a vast expanse of time and draws literature from people of faith in a variety of different cultures. As a result, the Bible responds to most questions about marriage with several answers rather than with only one. Consistently, though, the Bible regards marriage as a relationship of such spiritual significance that it can serve as a simile for God's relationship to people (Isa. 50:1; Jer. 2:1-2; Ezek. 16:23; Hos. 1–3) and Christ's relationship to the church (1 Cor. 11:3; Eph. 5:22-33).

Holy Scripture firmly fixes the foundation of marriage in creation, making it independent of culturally or ethnically conditioned laws. Marriage is a theological matter rather than a legal one. Law erroneously elevates the institution over individuals and fails to capture a full understanding of the marital relationship. In philosophical terminology, the ontological basis for marriage resides in creation and redemption, not in legislation.

To be sure, laws concerning marriage appear in the Old Testament. However, all these attempts legally to regulate marriage represent a concession necessitated by people's propensity to sin. As Jesus explained, the Mosaic law's provision for a divorce certificate stemmed from men's "hardness of heart" (Mark 10:5; Deut. 24:1-4) — people's moral weakness, in other words.

In the New Testament, marriage transcends law.[2] When confronted by questions about marriage and divorce, Jesus looked to creation as the

---

2. Helmut Thielicke, *The Ethics of Sex*, trans. John W. Doberstein (New York: Harper & Row, 1964), 108. Thielicke writes that a contemporary understanding of the meaning of marriage must be oriented to biblical factors that transcend the law "if they are to lay claim to being Christian interpretations."

source for his answers. Marriage is a spiritual provision from the eternal God, not a legal contract devised by historical personalities. Though Jesus spoke extensively about marriage on several different occasions, at no point did he intend for his words to be assigned the status of new legal statutes. He was exposing the weaknesses of old laws, not enacting new laws.[3]

When set in the context of creation and redemption, clearly the essence of marriage is a "one flesh" relationship between a man and a woman committed to each other for life. This kind of union rests on reciprocal promises of fidelity and involves shared purposes, thoughts, emotions, and goals as well as sex. Indeed, sexual union apart from these other dimensions of interpersonal unity fails to establish a marital relationship between a man and a woman. Marriage is a spiritual covenant.

So, when does marriage occur? What makes a marriage a marriage? What is the defining moment that transforms a relationship between a man and a woman into a marriage?

Unlike a book of codified law, the Bible does not concern itself with particulars that provide detailed answers for every conceivable question about marriage. Marriage is a one-flesh union between two people who promise fidelity to each other throughout their lives: that's it as far as the Bible is concerned. Marriage is a spiritual relationship, not the enactment of a carefully drawn legal contract.

We want to know more, though. Does marriage occur when a man and woman pledge themselves to each other in love? Or when the state recognizes their promises of fidelity? Or when the church acknowledges and blesses their pledges? Or when two people who have promised faithfulness to each other have sexual intercourse with each other for the first time? However, lacking a direct, explicit answer to each of these questions within the Bible, we are left to answer the inquiries on the basis of insights gleaned from the Bible.

Jesus described marriage as a permanent relationship of mutual commitment and intimate sharing. We know that for sure. Jesus discussed marital infidelity and adultery in terms of thoughts and desires as well as actions. Apparently, then, we best define both marriage and a betrayal

---

3. Thielicke comments on the nature of Jesus' words about marriage: "They can never become anything like constitutional principles for 'this world' or moral directions for life." He warns that Jesus' words "cannot be 'judified' or moralized" because they are "the corrective that calls in question, relativizes, and de-ideologizes all law and all morals." Thielicke, 116.

of marriage as matters of the heart — spiritual concerns related to promise making, promise keeping, and promise breaking. Without a doubt, that was the case in the Jewish view of marriage that prevailed at the time of Jesus.[4]

Among first-century Jews, a couple's exchange of promises in the "betrothal" that preceded their marriage ceremony (often by as long as a year) established a morally inviolable union between them.[5] With reference to matters of inheritance, adultery, and divorce, society treated a betrothed couple as married, though they did not yet live together. The union of their lives was established by their mutual promises of faithfulness and permanence regarding their marriage.

According to the New Testament, both marriage and adultery can occur apart from any physical sexual activity. A marital union precedes the sexual union of a couple. An episode of adultery can betray a marital relationship without sexual intercourse or sexual promiscuity of any kind on the part of one of the partners.[6] Marriage and adultery are matters of the heart as well as of the body — spiritual relationships before they are physical.

What's more, given Jesus' equation of lust with adultery, marital partners can violate each other morally even though they are legally married to each other and physically faithful to each other. Jesus identified both lust and adultery as desires (or actions) solely dedicated to self-gratification. Lust separates sex from love and treats a sexual partner as a thing rather than as a person. That can happen within a marriage! And it's wrong there as it is elsewhere. Marriage does not justify a couple treating each other as things and thus committing the sin that Jesus warned against in his association of lust with adultery.

A spiritual understanding of marriage sets up the possibility of another problem related to morality. Jesus clearly rejected the view that a sexual relationship between two people makes them a married couple

4. For a detailed description of the meaning of a betrothal and the nature of a marriage ceremony among first-century Jews, see Alfred Edersheim, *The Life and Times of Jesus the Messiah*, vol. 1 (Grand Rapids: Eerdmans, 1942), 148-50, 354-55.

5. "Unlawful intercourse with a woman betrothed to a man was adultery, because the betrothed woman was deemed as inviolable as the married woman." Punishment for this form of adultery was death by a public stoning. "Adultery," in *The Jewish Encyclopedia*, ed. Isidore Singer, vol. 1 (New York: Funk and Wagnalls, 1956), 217.

6. In a case of adultery, "the offender is liable under the law even if the intercourse were not completed; that is, took place without penetration." David M. Feldman, *Marital Relations, Birth Control and Abortion in Jewish Law* (New York: Schocken Books, 1974), 79.

(a concept at least implicit in Paul's suggestion in 1 Cor. 6:16 that a person can establish a one-flesh union with a prostitute). Vows of permanent fidelity, not sexual actions, establish a marriage. Turn the matter another way, though. What if a married person falls in love with someone outside the marriage and promises a fidelity of love, sexual relations, and permanent commitment to that individual? Does that constitute adultery or polygamy — a betrayal of the marriage, the creation of a new marriage, both, or neither?

My purpose is not to confuse the issue but to illustrate the difficulty of arriving at legalistic definitions for spiritual relationships and the ineptness of such definitions in solving moral dilemmas. Marriage is a spiritual covenant between two people. What, then, is adultery?

Adultery: Thought or Act

"Aw, come on," you say, "how difficult can it be to define adultery? Any fool knows that adultery means sexual intercourse between a married man and a married woman who are not married to each other."

Believe it or not, this classic definition of adultery proves inadequate as an accurate description of adulterous behavior. Cultural understandings of adultery differ substantially.[7] So do religious statements about an adulterous act. Even moral legalists find themselves in conflict about exactly what constitutes adultery.

The word "adultery" derives from the Latin *adulterare,* which means "to defile," and *adulterat(us),* which means "altered," which in turn come from *ad* and *alter ("different" or "other"). The word "adultery" describes a person going off to someone other than his wife or her husband.*[8]

As a designation of behavior, the word "adultery" carries moral and spiritual significance. It is a religious term that, since the early days

7. In her study of the natural history of adultery, Helen Fisher concludes that cultural mores dramatically affect people's definition of and attitude toward adultery. For example, traditional patriarchal societies, such as those of the Japanese, Chinese, Hindu, and preindustrial European people, viewed adultery primarily as a female vice. Seldom did anyone apply the word to men. Among the Kofyar people of Nigeria, marriage partners dissatisfied with each other but not wanting a divorce can take an extramarital lover into the home without being considered adulterous. Helen E. Fisher, *Anatomy of Love: The Natural History of Monogamy, Adultery, and Divorce* (New York: W. W. Norton, 1992), 78-79.

8. Annette Lawson, *Adultery: An Analysis of Love and Betrayal* (New York: Basic Books, 1988), 36-37.

of Judaism, people have associated with immorality or sin. However, even within the same religious tradition — the Judeo-Christian tradition — understandings of the precise behavior that constitutes the sin of adultery have varied considerably. And they still do.

One of the Ten Commandments, number seven to be precise, forbids adultery. The ancient imperative seems straightforward enough. As will be discussed below, however, this prohibition addressed a far more limited scope of behavior than many interpreters anticipate. Early Jewish moralists understood adultery primarily as a female sin, sexual intercourse between a married woman and someone else's husband. The evil of this union consisted of an offense against the woman's husband. Extramarital sexual involvements on the part of a man's wife violated that man's property rights, a serious offense. Thus, "Thou shalt not commit adultery."

Over an extended period of time, adultery as forbidden in the Decalogue took on a different, more expanded meaning. The word came to designate sexual intercourse between a married man and a married woman not married to each other. Influenced by this later development, contemporary Western morality considers adultery a moral transgression on the part of both the man and the woman involved in extramarital sexual relations.

Most legalists stop right here in addressing the subject of adultery. But that is a serious error. They stop short of the fullest understanding of adultery in the Jewish-Christian tradition. Within Judaism, adultery was a physical act. Refrain from coitus outside of marriage and you avoid the sin of adultery.[9] Not so in Christianity. Jesus applied the term "adultery" to attitudes as well as to acts, to a mind-set as well as to a physical deed — "Everyone who looks at a woman lustfully has already committed adultery with her in his heart" (Matt. 5:28).

Amazingly, many people within the Christian tradition fail to assign to the words of Jesus the same degree of importance they give to Old Testament words when it comes to discussions of adultery. Sex remains the crucial factor in their judgment, sexual intercourse specifically. Jesus viewed attitudinal sins and failures of the spirit far more severely than

---

9. An exception to this generally correct observation appears in a standard Jewish commentary. "It [the Seventh Commandment] involves the prohibition of immoral speech, immodest conduct, or associations with person who scoff at the sacredness of purity." J. H. Hertz, ed., *The Pentateuch and Haftorahs: Hebrew Text, English Translation and Commentary* (London: Soncino Press, 1981), 299.

acts of physical immorality. However, many contemporaries who call Jesus "Lord" condemn and often ostracize men and women accused (accurately or inaccurately) of extramarital sexual intercourse while not even addressing the mental and spiritual adultery that has reached epidemic proportions within their fellowships.

The situation is as understandable as it is wrong. As long as adultery can be defined narrowly, fewer people feel any guilt because of this sin. Regardless of the desires that burn in their hearts (or groins) and the wishes that fill their wills, many people see themselves as morally superior to individuals who actually have acted on their feelings. What would the church do if everybody was guilty of adultery? No one would be any better than anyone else! Perish the thought.

So, what is adultery? Obviously, the law fails to provide a satisfactory definition for adulterous behavior.

In the teachings of Jesus, the prohibition against adultery grew out of an affirmation of marriage — an appreciation for the God-willed durability of a covenant relationship between a husband and a wife. Sex alone was not the issue. Any thought, word, or act toward another person that violated the promises of fidelity embraced by an individual in the marriage vows constituted a form of adultery.

That much was understandable. But the Bible does not leave the issue there. Both Jesus and Paul stretched the definition of adultery still further.

Perhaps the most difficult-to-understand dimension of adultery arises from biblical statements largely ignored by all but the most conservative religious thinkers. Each of these scriptural texts addresses the subject of divorce and remarriage in such a manner as to postulate a new (and an additional) meaning to adultery.

First, a person commits adultery by divorcing a spouse only because of an interest in pursuing freedom (Mark 10:9). No extramarital sexual activities have to be involved for such a divorce to constitute adultery. Any individual who forces a divorce for personal reasons repudiates the permanent marriage bond intended by God and demonstrates a lack of commitment to the one-flesh nature of marriage.

Second, a person who receives a divorce and subsequently remarries commits adultery (Mark 10:11; Rom. 7:3). Given the indissolubility of the marriage bond, as much of the Bible teaches, a second marriage betrays the first marriage and thus constitutes an act of adultery.

Third, a person divorced by a spouse even against her own will commits adultery (Mark 10:11). This individual does not become involved in adultery voluntarily, but as a result of the actions of the divorcing spouse. According to this point of view, no "innocent" party exists in the breakup of a marriage.

Finally, a third party, even if the third party is a person who has never been married, commits adultery by marrying an individual who has been divorced (Luke 16:18). The seemingly innocent newlywed commits a sin by participating in a relationship with a person still morally bound to an indissoluble first union.

Little, if any, of the recent, non-religiously oriented literature on adultery even considers the issues of divorce and remarriage as relevant topics. The prevailing point of view understands adultery only in terms of extramarital sexual involvement. However, innumerable people tutored within the Christian church chafe at the charge and grapple with the guilt that develop by associating divorce and remarriage with adultery.

Actually, many marriage therapists have ceased using the word "adultery" with their clients. They dislike the term because of the inadequacy of its legalistically defined content and because its usage immediately conveys a negative moral judgment. Most counselors with this mentality prefer to speak of affairs or infidelity rather than adultery. In reality, their replacement language may get closer to the Bible's essential concern about adultery (as reflected in the teachings of Jesus, not in the Ten Commandments) than can be accomplished by the word "adultery" itself.

At issue in adultery is a personal involvement that violates that person's commitment to his or her marital partner and thus threatens the durability of a marriage. Sexual intercourse may have taken place in the extramarital relationship, but not necessarily. Whether or not coitus has occurred, if the psychophysical fellowship of a marriage has been interrupted by another psychophysical experience, the problem is adultery.[10] Call it what you wish.

Whether or not a person agrees with any or with all of these definitions of adultery, everyone who reads them confronts an emphatic declaration of the importance of marriage. The Bible's views on adultery especially point to the primacy of a durable marital relationship. Even not necessarily biblical views of adultery implicitly affirm the importance of fidelity within marriage.

10. Thielicke, 259.

At this point we have to acknowledge that neither marriage nor adultery can be defined legalistically, at least as far as the Bible is concerned. Both marriage and adultery are matters of the heart (as well as of the body). That lack of meticulous certainty causes some people great anxiety. Abiding by the letter of the law does not assure authentic moral integrity. What, then, are we to conclude about morality generally and sin specifically?

Sin: Physical or Spiritual

Everybody knows what sin is. Or do they? Frequently people confuse symptoms of sin (often called "sins") and the substance of sin. Add to that misunderstanding popular misconceptions of the Bible's teaching about flesh (or the body), with their consequent tendency to equate evil with all that is physical, and a problem arises, a serious problem that adversely impacts how people define sin and respond to sinners.

Though the Bible contains many different terms for "sin," a singular definition of sin prevails. The essence of sin is rebellion against God, revolt against the divine will. Sin can be described in a variety of ways: missing the mark, violating the holy, erring morally, living lawlessly, disobeying God, functioning selfishly, practicing unrighteousness, taking life into your own hands. But all of these descriptions of sin point to the same reality — revolt against God.[11]

Sin denotes a condition more than an action — a spiritual condition. People who sin push God to the periphery of life, if not ignore God completely. To determine the reality of sin in a person requires not an inventory of activities (what the individual has or has not done) but a concept of identity (who the person is in relation to God; whether the individual lives in communion with God or in rebellion against God).

By the way, no reason exists to spend time and energy seeking to determine the presence of sin in another person's life. The Bible clearly indicates that sin resides in all of us.

But what about sins? What we commonly call sins represent symptoms of sin, dead giveaways of the dominance of sin — consequences of taking life into our own hands and living as if God did not matter. Thus dishonesty, thievery, profanity, and, yes, adultery point to a spiritual

---

11. Leander E. Keck, *Paul and His Letters* (Philadelphia: Fortress Press, 1979), 117-28.

condition properly termed "sinful." But no one of these sinful traits of personal behavior exceeds another in severity. All point to the same condition — rebellion against God.

Sometimes the clarity of a definition can be enhanced by placing it against a negative backdrop. What sin *is* — what sin means — becomes more apparent by recognizing what sin *is not* — what sin does not mean.

Sin is not a physical act. The source of such a possibility resides more in the heresy of gnosticism than in orthodox Christianity. Gnostics positioned flesh and spirit against each other, equating spirit with good and flesh with evil. According to gnostic thought, the spirit of a person (the dimension of life most in touch with God) is trapped in flesh (a person's physical body), which lures the person away from a relationship with God. Salvation, then, consists of freeing the spirit (or soul) from the body.

No such antithetical relationship between body and spirit can be found in the Bible. Indeed, Christianity centers on Incarnation — the Word become flesh, a revelation of the holy God through a physical being. The apostle Paul addressed this matter in great detail.

Paul used the term "flesh" to describe human nature — not a lower form of nature, but human nature. Though at times Paul pitted spirit and flesh against each other, he did not equate flesh and sin. In the mind of the apostle, battles between flesh and spirit represented struggles between "the power of the eschatalogical future and the power of the empirical present,"[12] not a war between the drives of the body and the desires of the spirit. As a matter of fact, Paul considered a person's body as a person's self. Thus, a person's body possessed significance in relationship to God even as did an individual's spirit.

Even when Paul used the word "flesh" with an obviously negative connotation, he did not associate evil exclusively with the physical. Take, for example, what the apostle called "works of the flesh" (Gal. 5:19-21). Out of fifteen such works, only five of them are in any way physical. The others involve thoughts and emotions as well as personal will.[13]

Most people (in both church and society) reserve their harshest

---

12. Keck, 108. Frank Stagg understands "flesh" as representative of a whole person apart from redemption and "spirit" as representative of a whole person under redemption. Frank Stagg, "Freedom and Moral Responsibility Without License or Legalism," *Review and Expositor* 64, no. 4 (1972): 489.

13. L. H. Marshall, *The Challenge of New Testament Ethics* (London: MacMillan, 1964), 37, 41.

judgments for physical acts of wrongdoing — especially physical actions involving sex. Adultery usually tops the list of immoral repugnances, while emotions and attitudes such as anger, pride, self-righteousness, and judgment hardly get considered as wrong at all. Terminology betrays the popular sentiment. A "morals charge" suggests an act of illicit or illegal sexual behavior, as if "morals" involved only sexuality.

Jesus was different. In fact, the Messiah played havoc with traditional lists of virtues and sins in both the church and society. In contrast to the prevailing view of great wrongs, Jesus looked most unfavorably on expressions of temper. Though he never condoned sexual immorality, Jesus consistently responded to persons caught up in sexual immorality with mercy. While he treated sinful expressions of temper with "withering denunciation," Jesus treated outcroppings of sexual passion with pity.[14]

Harshly judging two people guilty of sexual misconduct represents rebellion against God — sin — just as does the wrongdoing judged. Sin is a spiritual condition.

Is there no place for judgment, then? What does "judgment" mean?

Judgment: Retribution or Redemption

Judgment receives mixed reviews. Responsible moralists passionately devoted to respectability commend judgment as a mark of exemplary wisdom. Not so Jesus, though. Jesus admonished people to avoid judgment like a plague (Matt. 7:1).

What is the deal here? How can judgments about judgment vary so dramatically, especially among persons who care about morality? What is judgment? What is its purpose?

The New Testament word translated "to judge" *(krino)* means "to decide." However, the process of deciding (making up one's mind, choosing between alternatives, or forming an opinion) involves far more than discretion. Reaching a judgment *(krisis)* results in division, separation, and condemnation. New Testament writers used "judgment" and "condemnation" interchangeably, as synonyms (see Rom. 2:1).

---

14. George Buttrick observed that Jesus brought "upheaval in our list of sins.... Sins of the passions have darkly crowned the list; whereas jealousy, anger, pride and harsh judgment have hardly been counted sins. ... Jesus treated sins of passion with pity. ... He never condoned such guilt or minimized it. But He met it with mercy." George A. Buttrick, *The Parables of Jesus* (New York: Harper & Row, 1928), 195-96.

"Surely we must make moral judgments," protests a person sincerely concerned about an erosion of basic values and fearful of endorsing ethical irresponsibility. Yes, of course. Conscientious moral analysis is far superior to flabby indifference about moral issues. Individuals who evaluate the morality of their words and actions, along with the motivations and consequences of both, nurture healthy personal and social sensitivity. Without question, such moral discretion (judgment) deserves praise.

Value-oriented reflection contributes to clarity, wisdom, and a capacity to distinguish between destructive and constructive behavior. Self-evaluations of moral postures greatly enhance the possibility of sound decisions related to good and evil. Making moral judgments about other people is a completely different matter, though.

As forewarned by the linguistic heritage of the word "judgment," an act of judgment regarding others expresses condemnation, spawns division, and reeks havoc with hopes for salvation. Take a bad situation, inject into it people predisposed to judging others, and invariably the situation worsens.

No one benefits from condemnation — neither the condemned nor the condemner. A person passing judgment on another individual may for a brief moment derive an emotional high from a sense of moral superiority over the individual condemned. However, that false sensation quickly fades. A close scrutiny of the judgments we make about other people inevitably brings us face-to-face with a hurtful judgment about ourselves.[15]

A craving to pass judgment on others often stems from a ravenous hunger for personal security. Here's how it works. Establishing ourselves as the judge of another person's behavior endows us with a sense of power and control. After all, a judge determines right and wrong for everybody

15. Students of personal behavior argue that individuals' judgments of others relate directly to the troublesome concerns that those individuals harbor about themselves. Most people tend to play out their personal guilt and tendencies toward self-punishment in the arena of other people's lives. John Jacob Raub writes, "Others and situations become for us the arena where we play out our inner sense of guilt and self-punishment." John Jacob Raub, *Who Told You That You Were Naked? Freedom from Judgment, Guilt and Fear of Punishment* (New York: Crossroad, 1993), 47. Similarly, Peter McWilliams observes, "If we move from the *action* we judge, and look at the *judgment*, we usually find a similar judgment we make about ourselves." Peter McWilliams, *Love 101: To Love Oneself Is the Beginning of a Lifelong Romance* (Los Angeles: Prelude Press, 1995), 85.

and makes those who disagree with that judgment pay dearly. A certain elevation of one's self accompanies a moral condemnation of someone else. ("I may not be all that great, but at least I am better than he is.")

In matters of security, relinquishing judgment means losing control. Stripped of the power to pronounce judgments about other people, we risk the possibility of wrongdoers receiving forgiveness rather than punishment and benefiting from a far more generous extension of mercy than we feel is fair. Fear develops — a fear that if we can't judge other people, the moral universe may spin out of control or disintegrate. What an awesome burden to carry. *"God is counting on us,"* some people think in a panic. *"We know morality and we must enforce high morals."*

Strange how some folks want to be more moral than God — or so it seems! Jesus said God does not judge (John 5:22).

Jesus could have appealed to our lack of competence to pass judgments as the basis for his warning "Do not judge." None of us knows another person well enough to judge that person. What's more, none of us knows enough about God to voice God's response to an individual caught in wrongdoing.

In his parables on judgment, Jesus demonstrated how God looks at a sinful person much differently than do most people. In story after story, Jesus turned morality on its head. He abolished the standard criteria by which people commonly make judgments about each other and established salvation as the goal of judgment. Jesus envisioned the crisis of judgment *(krisis)* as an opportunity for people to experience acceptance and inclusion.[16]

Jesus prohibited judgment because condemnation works at cross-purposes with salvation. Judgment foments division, alienation, and condemnation, actions in opposition to salvation. Salvation creates forgiveness, reconciliation, restoration, and communion. God prefers salvation.

Once we have passed judgment on another person's behavior, we find it virtually impossible to respond to that person with even a minimal measure of life-giving help. We shut down love and suggest the death of hope by separating the judged person from the presence of God. Our judgment — condemnation — erects a barrier between a bad situation and the salvation — acceptance, inclusion, and freedom — that God desires to offer all involved in that situation.

16. Robert Farrar Capon, *The Mystery of Christ . . . and Why We Don't Get It* (Grand Rapids: Eerdmans, 1993), 87.

Jesus left no doubt about God's posture toward sinners. The Gospel of John declares, "For God sent the Son into the world, not to condemn the world, but that the world might be saved through him" (John 3:17). God responds to sinners with an offer of salvation, not with a declaration of judgment. Why would followers of Jesus, or anyone else for that matter, opt for another way?

Most people think of judgment (both the process of deciding and the decision made) as a prelude to punishment. However, Jesus eradicated this purpose of judgment. He revealed God's desire for forgiveness and salvation, not sentencing and punishment, in response to sinners. No wonder judgment disappears from all lists of religious priorities based on the ministry of Jesus.

"This is crazy!" comes a loud complaint. The sound of the protest signals incredulous impatience that has finally exploded. Well, maybe God's preference for salvation rather than condemnation is crazy. From the perspective of classic jurisprudence, it certainly appears illogical. The legal system metes out punishment proportionate to the seriousness of every act judged as wrong. And, make no mistake about it, the purpose of that punishment is retribution, not redemption. A similar opinion holds sway in most traditional theologies. Sin invites judgment, which requires punishment. Martin Luther correctly observed, "If you follow human reason [i.e., human justice], you are forced to say either there is no God, or that God is unjust."[17] If logic requires that every sin be condemned and punished, then God's sovereign presence creates a realm of craziness. Where God rules, justice gives way to grace.

A lot of people have major problems with this kind of God. As Robert Farrar Capon observes, we typically want "a nasty-nice little judge who will keep crimes against faith off the streets."[18] God disappoints such an expectation because of a relentless passion for people's salvation. Biased by love, God views a crisis of wrongdoing as an opportunity for something good to happen. To people hurting because of their sins, God brings compassion, not condemnation; pity, not retribution; fellowship, not separation.

Most of us cannot even comprehend a nonjudgmental fellowship, much less a noncondemning world — the very goal toward which God

---

17. Raub, 59.
18. Robert Farrar Capon, *The Parables of Judgment* (Grand Rapids: Eerdmans, 1989), 151.

calls us. The Gospel of Luke describes God as "kind to the ungrateful and the selfish" (Luke 6:35). No matter how incomprehensible to us, kindness to the wicked constitutes a distinctive trait of God.[19]

An investigation of the biblical meaning of judgment leads to the conclusion that God's only purpose is to save. Any lingering idea of judgment as retribution goes up in the smoke that rises from the fire of God's love.

With our prejudices about judgment and punishment in shambles and our view of God stretched to new depths of adoration, we had best inquire about the meaning of salvation.

Salvation: Inclusive or Exclusive

Linguistically, "salvation" means "a roomy place, a spacious area."[20] To be saved is to be removed from confinement in a narrow context and set in a large place. Theologically, salvation means deliverance by God.[21] To be saved is to be rescued from an oppressive, deadly situation and ushered into the bountiful goodness of a loving relationship with God. Experientially, salvation means freedom. To be saved is to be set free to become the persons we were created to be. Linguistically, theologically, and experientially, salvation denotes the reception of assistance — unmerited assistance, biblically speaking. Being saved differs from anything people can achieve for themselves. The source of salvation resides beyond the realm of humankind.

Most people agree that God is in the business of salvation. Disputes arise, however, as people try to designate *who* is eligible for salvation and *when.*

Some folks contend that God offers salvation only to individuals who merit it. Various suggestions have been made regarding the merit that invites salvation: a record of good deeds, a proper statement of repentance, the purchase of an indulgence, repetition of a stylized con-

19. Raub, 69.

20. For a careful analysis of the linguistic history of the word "salvation," see Werner Foerster and Georg Fohrer, *"sozo, soteria, soter, soterios,"* in *Theological Dictionary of the New Testament,* vol. 7, ed. Gerhard Kittel and Gerhard Friedrich, trans. Geoffrey W. Bromiley (Grand Rapids: Eerdmans, 1971), 965-1024.

21. For a thorough discussion of salvation as an act of deliverance, see Alan Richardson, "Salvation, Savior," in *The Interpreter's Dictionary of the Bible,* vol. 4, ed. George Arthur Buttrick (Nashville: Abingdon Press, 1962), 168-81.

fession, an interest in the institutional church, the enactment of a religious ritual, a commitment to a particular pattern of morality. Within this perspective, salvation depends on the words and actions of people desiring salvation and becomes an exclusive rather than an inclusive experience.

Jesus forcefully challenged this concept of salvation. Using the imagery of illness and health, Jesus observed that sick people, not well people, need a doctor (Mark 2:17). Similarly, individuals in trouble, not persons for whom all is well, need salvation. Deliverance from bondage into freedom has importance only for people in captivity, not for liberated persons already enjoying freedom. To make accessibility to salvation dependent on people's ability to get their lives in order robs salvation of its most fundamental meaning. In other words, salvation is for sinners. Who else?

Suggestions that salvation arrives in a person's life only when that person ceases to sin — heaven help us if that is the case! — run counter to the message of the New Testament. By way of three popular parables (see Luke 15), Jesus described lostness as the one prerequisite for salvation. Only a lost coin, a lost sheep, and a lost son can be found.

Interestingly, Jesus recognized no variations in lostness. He made no distinction between an inescapable lostness and lostness as an avoidable consequence of foolishness, irresponsibility, meanness, or intentional selfishness. Jesus responded to all forms of lostness with the good news of God's salvation.

God's salvation is inclusive: for everyone. God extends salvation to people who know firsthand hurt, need, helplessness, and alienation. Refusing to delay redemptive action until we become respectable, God embraces us with love even while we appear unlovable. Biblically speaking, God does not save us *from* sin but *in* sin. God does not deliver us *from* failure but *in* failure. The apostle Paul stated the situation most clearly: "God shows his love for us in that while we were yet sinners Christ died for us" (Rom. 5:8).

Attempts to turn God's gift to everybody into a badge of merit, a payoff, or a reward for only a few represents the worst antics of religion, not the essence of Christianity. Tragically, religion often takes what God makes available as the basis for communion — salvation — and turns it into a cause for division.

Think again of the lifelike, though fictional, account of Hester Prynne. Self-declared religious people ostracized Hester and separated themselves from her by making her sin a cause for division. How ironic. At the moment of the woman's greatest need for fellowship and assistance, religious people condemned her, set her apart from help, and increased her burden by forcing her to wear a badge of shame. A truly saving community, wasn't it? The early Puritans described by Hawthorne wanted to restrict the availability of salvation to morally respectable people, to offer salvation only to individuals who really didn't need it. Such bad theology continues to attract a huge following and to inspire hurtful actions.

God offers salvation to everybody. No exceptions. God extends the possibility of salvation to all the Hester Prynnes of the world as well as to all akin to her persecutors. Honestly, though, the Hester types have a much better shot at experiencing salvation than do their critics, because of a realistic recognition and a truthful admission of their need for salvation.

Often persons who affirm the possibility of salvation for all sinners attempt to stipulate when salvation can and cannot occur. According to this point of view, God delivers individuals from lostness only one time. After that, everyone is on their own. And they'd better not sin.

When sin occurs and troubles arise in the life of a person who has been saved — as inevitably happens — proponents of limited salvation say, "Tough luck. You knew better. No help is available." Sadly, such folks confuse meanness and righteousness.

Jesus offered unlimited salvation, the kind of salvation that God had made possible for people since the very first act of divine deliverance. According to the Old Testament record, how many times did God deliver the same people from forms of bondage that, in every instance, they could have avoided? Faithful to this tradition, Jesus taught what he practiced — that forgiveness has no limits and salvation no restrictions.

Jesus answered the *when* question about salvation in the same way he responded to the *who* inquiry about salvation. No limits, no exceptions. The only unforgivable act a person can commit is a relentless refusal to accept God's offer of forgiveness, an outright rejection of God's acceptance.

"But mustn't a person try to do better and promise not to need God's deliverance again?" I sense someone straining to ask. No. God refuses to make salvation conditional on promises of reform. However, God's deliverance sets in motion dynamics that inspire reform and make it possible.[22]

---

22. Robert Farrar Capon, *Between Noon and Three: A Parable of Romance, Law, and the Outrage of Grace* (San Francisco: Harper & Row, 1982), 112.

Salvation as the gift of God's deliverance into freedom is an amazing thing — so amazing that it makes many people uncomfortable. The beauty of this salvation is that God graciously sets up as the only prerequisite for receiving it the only thing none of us will ever be without — sin and the need for deliverance that sin causes.[23] God's provision of salvation inspires a shout of invitation, "Come one, come all!"

Defining the terms of our dialogue is a good discipline. Obviously, however, definitions alone do not bring about unanimity among opinions.

A sense of direction develops in an elaboration of definitions, even a hunch as to the answer to the forgiveness question about adultery. God desires forgiveness and salvation for everybody, no exceptions. Acts of adultery represent serious sins, but not unforgivable sins — in fact, sins no worse than the sins of those who bombard adulterers with judgment and condemnation while withholding from them forgiveness and promises of help and hope. God's love and grace will not be deterred by acts of infidelity — physical, emotional, or spiritual.

Before we come to a more specific conclusion on adultery, however, more research is in order. We need to take a look at the Bible's teachings related to this matter. What better place to start than with a study of the divine commandments?

COMMANDMENTS IN CONFLICT

A psychedelic bumper sticker declares: "God said it. I believe it. That settles it." Similarly, a popular mind-set, impatient with ambiguity and passionate for simplicity, avows, "The Bible means exactly what it says. Commandments carry no subtleties. God has mandated what we are to do and not to do. We must obey God's commandments or suffer the consequences of disobedience. It's just that simple."

Individuals driven by a penchant for certainty usually maintain a very narrow focus. In relation to moral law, they tend to look at only one commandment at a time, refusing to deal with problems that arise when several different commandments interact with one another ("What should we do when obedience to one commandment jeopardizes our

23. Robert Farrar Capon, *The Parables of Grace* (Grand Rapids: Eerdmans, 1988), 86.

obedience to another commandment?"). Difficulties in understanding ensue.

Preoccupation with a single commandment in the Bible to the exclusion of the entire sweep of scriptural truth leaves important questions unanswered: Is one commandment more important than all others? If so, which one? Do the Ten Commandments represent the whole of Christian morality? Does a statement from Jesus carry more authority and merit more attention than a piece of legislation lifted from the Jewish moral code? Does disobedience to a commandment carry with it the certainty of punishment, or do the people of God have a responsibility to punish all who break divine laws? What is the proper response to a person who breaks one of the Ten Commandments in light of Jesus' instructions to treat sinners with love and grace?

The Purpose of Commandments

Understanding the nature and purpose of divine commandments aids a discovery of correct answers to these inquiries. A hint at such understanding inheres in the prologue to the Ten Commandments — "I am the Lord your God, who brought you out of the land of Egypt, out of the house of bondage" (Exod. 20:2). That statement embodies pure love and marvelous grace. The God who sets down commandments acts out of love. Grace and unmerited favor make up the heart of God's nature. Thus, all God's prohibitions represent revelations of compassion. God offers commandments to enhance, not to restrict life.

God desires for people to experience life at its best. So, as a lover longing for everybody to know the joyful liberation that springs from truth telling, God commands people not to lie. As a grace-giver seeking to direct humankind toward physical rest and spiritual health, God commands individuals to observe a Sabbath Day each week.

Controversy swirled around Jesus because of his attitude regarding commandments. Within Judaism, no institution rivaled the Sabbath in importance. Respect for the Sabbath was rooted in obedience to one of the Ten Commandments. Though Jesus respected the Sabbath and recognized the moral need for rest and worship, he did not allow Sabbath laws to prohibit him from doing the work of love and grace on Sabbath days. Jewish legalists grew livid watching Jesus on the Sabbath and accused him of breaking the law. In his response to these critics, Jesus made no effort to invalidate the Sabbath commandment;

he just reached behind it to grasp (and act on) the divine love that inspired it. To the dismay of many of his peers, Jesus explained, "The sabbath was made for man, not man for the sabbath" (Mark 2:27).

Jesus' statements popularly known as "the beatitudes" (Matt. 5:2-12) explicitly reassert the divine intention behind moral laws such as those found in the Ten Commandments. The master teacher couched each of his comments in mercy and oriented it toward happiness. Jesus wanted his disciples to know how best to enjoy life. So, through the beatitudes, Jesus pointed to the joy of hungering and thirsting after righteousness, practicing mercy, and making peace, just as God earlier through the Decalogue had pointed to the goodness of life that can be experienced when people honor their parents, tell the truth, and remain faithful to the marriage covenant.

Love and grace constitute the foundation of God's commandments, the intention of which is life enhancement. Thus, the purpose of God's commandments gets distorted severely when people wield the divinely given moral mandates as weapons to injure persons and reduce the joy of life. Of course, God desires obedience to the moral law. But God finds as much displeasure in people who use a person's moral lapses as occasions to inflict hurt, assure unrelieved guilt, and shut doors to a meaningful future for that person as in the disobedient individual. Such actions violate the grace that stands behind the law that was broken. And to betray grace is a sin every bit as grievous as breaking the law (if not more so).

The Seventh Commandment

You shall not commit adultery.

(Exodus 20:14)

According to the Bible, amid thunder, lightning, fire, and smoke atop Mount Sinai, God entrusted to Moses, a Jewish patriarch, two tablets of stone on which the essence of moral legislation mysteriously had been inscribed. In "the Ten Words" (the Decalogue) the creator God declared how the highest order of creation should live. God instructed people how to live religiously, socially, and personally. Each law appeared as a prohibition. All the laws carried a universal application.

Second among the divine mandates on interpersonal relations stood a negation of adulterous behavior. Other statutes in the Bible similarly forbid adultery. The severity of the prohibition against adultery becomes starkly apparent in the nature of the punishment prescribed for people who disobey it — death (Lev. 20:10, Deut. 22:22).

What God intends in a revelation of the divine will and what people interpret God's disclosure to mean can differ significantly. Without claiming in any way to know the mind of God (an audacious assumption for anyone), I suspect that the adultery commandment received a less-than-God-intended interpretation, at least initially. Jesus certainly gave the ancient prohibition a tradition-breaking interpretation and application of immense proportions.

The people first confronted with the seventh commandment considered adultery a female sin, which violated a husband's property right and raised questions about the legitimacy of his offspring.[24] Judgments about adultery arose exclusively from a masculine point of view — "My wife is my property, and a taboo to all other men."[25]

Old Testament writers depicted adultery as a form of murder.[26] The statement of the Ten Commandments that appears in Deuteronomy makes that association abundantly clear. There the writer linguistically linked adultery with murder as forbidden in the prohibition immediately preceding it (Deut. 5:17-18). Adultery robbed a husband of his selfhood, a robbery considered a form of murder.

Most early Jews deemed adultery a "heinous crime" (Job 31:11). However, early on, no one equated adultery with total moral depravity or a violation of sexual morality.[27] After King David's adulterous relationship with Bathsheba, Yahweh threatened to give David's wives to other men (2 Sam. 12:11).

A more profound understanding of the evil addressed by the seventh commandment developed as adultery became a symbol for religious disloyalty. Idol worship among the people of Israel adulterated Jehovah worship, dumped impurities into an activity that had been

---

24. Henry H. Shires and Pierson Parker, "The Book of Deuteronomy," in *The Interpreter's Bible*, vol. 2, ed. George Arthur Buttrick (Nashville: Abingdon Press, 1952), 368. Note the exception in note 9 above.

25. J. Edgar Park, "The Book of Exodus," in *The Interpreter's Bible*, vol. 1, ed. George Arthur Buttrick (Nashville: Abingdon Press, 1952), 987.

26. Otto A. Piper, *The Biblical View of Sex and Marriage* (New York: Charles Scribner's Sons, 1960), 150; Earl F. Palmer, *Old Law New Life: The Ten Commandments and New Testament Faith* (Nashville: Abingdon Press, 1984), 105ff.

27. Shires and Parker, 368.

clean.[28] Prophets used the terms "adultery" and "infidelity" synony-
mously in their oracles. Adultery was (and is) a sin of betrayal.

But what about sex? In contemporary society, talk of adultery
revolves around the subject of sex almost singularly. By definition, the
Decalogue's declaration against adultery prohibited sexual intercourse
between a married or an engaged woman and someone other than her
husband or fiancé. Adultery involved sex — sexual union between two
married people who were not married to each other. However, adulterous behavior embraced far more than extramarital sexual activities.

Jesus spoke of adultery as a sin that could occur apart from a sexual
union between two people. Reasserting what must have been the original
substance of God's prohibition, Jesus declared that thoughts and wishes
could qualify as adultery just as did extramarital sexual intercourse (Matt.
5:27-28).

The words of Jesus reveal the inadequacy of a strict, legalistic
approach to morality generally and to adultery specifically. Judged by
the letter of the law, two persons can link their lives in an extramarital
affair involving all the elements of lovemaking — rational sharing,
emotional bonding, sexual play — but stop just short of coitus and not
commit adultery. Such behavior, however, blatantly violates the spirit of
the seventh commandment. Jesus stressed the comprehensive intent of
the prohibition against adultery, insisting on thoughts and actions that
preserve and strengthen the marriage covenant.

A serious study of Jesus' teaching about adultery produces important conclusions about the sin of adultery and the seventh commandment, which counsels avoidance of it. First, everybody is guilty of this
wrong. Everybody! Of course, not all married people have engaged in
sexual intercourse with an individual other than their spouse. But what
married person has not entertained an adulterous thought, fed an adulterous fantasy, or sustained an adulterous stare? Keep in mind that Jesus
made little distinction between an adulterous thought and an adulterous
act. No person legitimately can claim the moral purity required to look
down on another individual regarding the sin of adultery.

Second, the seventh commandment affirms marriage and opposes
all that destroys a marriage (whether from inside the marriage or from
outside of it). People never guilty of a sexual union outside their marriage

28. David A. Seamands, *God's Blueprint for Living: New Perspectives on the Ten Commandments* (Wilmore, KY: Bristol Books, 1988), 103.

can violate the substance of the adultery commandment in numerous other ways. Any act that weakens trust and contributes to dishonesty (emotional or oral) within a marriage qualifies as adultery. Even sexual activities between a husband and wife can be adulterous in nature if they are devoid of complete psychophysical giving and receiving. Obedience to the seventh commandment requires far more than negative success — avoiding physical infidelity in relation to a marriage partner. This declaration in the Decalogue demands positive success — a husband and wife nurturing a healthy, durable relationship with each other.

Finally, the importance of the seventh commandment equals, but does not transcend, the importance of the other nine commandments. Without question, adultery is wrong. So are lying, stealing, and breaking the principle of Sabbath rest. Repeatedly, Jesus dealt with sins of the spirit more harshly than he did sins of the flesh. A "morals" charge against a person can be leveled as appropriately in reaction to ruinous gossip and destructive judgment as for extramarital sex. For followers of Jesus, all kinds of sins are serious. And all kinds of sin are forgivable.

This third observation raises still more important questions. Is one commandment more important than another? If so, which one? And why? Jesus addressed those questions. His answers to them merit careful attention.

The Great Commandment

"The first is, 'Hear, O Israel: The Lord our God, the Lord is one; and you shall love the Lord your God with all your heart, and with all your mind, and with all your strength.' The second is this, 'You shall love your neighbor as yourself.' There is no other commandment greater than these."

(Mark 12:29-31)

Early rabbis debated the relative importance of the commandments, ranking them from the "weightiest" to the "lightest." No wonder. First-century Judaism recognized 613 commandments — 365 negative and 248 positive. (Negatives always seem to outweigh positives.) Naturally, people wanted to know if certain commandments should receive priority attention or if they were all of equal importance.

Eventually a question of that nature was put to Jesus — "Which commandment is the first of all?" (Mark 12:28). The Gospel of Mark probably provides the earliest account of the conversation that ensued.[29] In a statement that continues to unsettle legalists, Jesus brought together two commandments seldom, if ever, brought together before. He placed them on equal footing and declared that together they formed the greatest of all the commandments in the Old Testament.

Though other people had offered summations of the law long before Jesus, no one had interpreted the law as Jesus did. Rabbinic comparisons of the commandments aimed at finding a basic principle from which the rest of the law could be deduced as a corollary. The rabbis wanted every commandment obeyed. Jesus, however, indicated that if people obeyed the essential thrust of the law as summarized in the great commandment, attentiveness to the remainder of the commandments was not important. Jesus demonstrated more concern for challenging people to embody the spirit of God's Word than for rearranging commandments or revising the law. Jesus rejected any legalism that could hinder people from acting according to God's will for love.

Answering a lawyer's question about the greatest of all the commandments in Judaism, Jesus brought together statements from Deuteronomy 6:5 — "You shall love the Lord your God with all your heart, and with all your soul, and with all your might" — and Leviticus 19:18 — "You shall love your neighbor as yourself." Designating the latter injunction as a "second" commandment indicated only that obedience to it depended on a person's compliance with the former commandment.

If adultery was (is) the gravest and most reprehensible of sins, surely Jesus would have mentioned it immediately when asked to specify the most important commandment in the Old Testament. You would expect the most important commandment to prohibit the worst of sins. Jesus did not repeat the prohibition against adultery in that situation because adultery is not an exceptional sin that merits a more severe response than that due to any other sin.

Jesus' statement elevated considerations of God-pleasing morality to a new high. People eager to learn what actions most pleased God learned that no number of personal actions could fulfill God's requirements for them. God desires the gift of every individual's total per-

---

29. Vincent Taylor, *The Gospel According to St. Mark: The Greek Text with Introduction, Notes, and Indexes,* 2nd ed. (New York: St. Martin's Press, 1976), 484.

sonality, whole being. A satisfactory relationship with God consists of compassionate devotion rather than prescribed obedience, love rather than legalism.

Any Jewish person serious about faith readily understood the meaning of the injunction to love God. Jesus lifted this part of the great commandment straight out of the Shema, the Old Testament confession that pious Jews recited daily (Deut. 6:4). Loving God means relating to God with the total devotion of one's heart, soul, and might—in other words, the gift of an individual's entire personality. Biblical morality consists of loving God rather than keeping a law, though the two should not be mutually exclusive.

No doubt, the most shocking dimension of Jesus' response to the lawyer's question was his elevation of the commandment of neighbor love to a status of importance equal to that of the mandate to love God. Most of the people who first heard Jesus' words harbored confusion about exactly who qualified as their neighbor. Thus, few of them knew as much about how to love their neighbors as how to love God. These people must have been staggered by Jesus' insistence that true love for God finds expression in true love for one's neighbor. His point could hardly be missed—a person cannot love God and hate her neighbor.

In the commandment commended by Jesus, a person's love for himself served as the pattern for loving his neighbor. The setting of the ancient Levitical commandment provides additional insight into the nature of this kind of love. Neighbor-love informed by self-love actively promotes the neighbor's good and aggressively acts to assure the neighbor's well-being. Such love stands in sharp contrast to bearing ill will against a neighbor, hating a neighbor, or acting with vengeance toward a neighbor.

Jesus even gave new meaning to the concept of *neighbor*. Within Old Testament Judaism, neighbor always meant another Jew—only another Jew. In Jewish thought, a non-Jew failed to qualify as a neighbor. Jesus broadened the meaning of the term "neighbor" to include Gentiles as well as Jews. Beyond that, Jesus identified one's neighbor as anyone in need of help.

In Luke, the parable of the good Samaritan immediately follows the narrative that parallels Mark's account of Jesus' comments on the great commandment. This popular story elaborates the rather unpopular definition of "neighbor" voiced by Jesus. A person's neighbor is anyone in a ditch. Anyone! Obviously, then, obedience to the great commandment requires extending help both to people shoved into a ditch by others and to persons whose own behavior caused them to wind up in a ditch — for example, victims of robberies and casualties of adultery.

The way Jesus summarized the law negated legalism as a proper means of relating to God and to other people. In fact, legal prescriptions (conformity to other commandments or a lack of conformity to them) can no longer be used to determine a person's closeness to or distance from the reign of God. Only actions prompted by love properly fulfill God's will. Love-based behavior constitutes the "better righteousness" that Jesus talked about so much.

The practical application of Jesus' judgment about the great commandment seems self-evident. The most telltale aspects of a person's character are the nature of that person's love for God and the existence (or lack of it) of that individual's compassionate actions on behalf of people in trouble. Jesus sets up the disturbing possibility that an adulterer in love with God can actually be more in conformity to the reign of God than a moral perfectionist who has kept all the legal mandates about not lying, not stealing, not committing adultery, and not cursing, but failed to offer God's kind of help to an adulterer. Anyone who deems that observation to be merely theoretical and highly questionable needs only look at the difference between the manner in which Jesus responded to an adulteress caught in the act and the way he reacted to the people who were ready to stone this woman to death rather than help her get on with her life (John 7:53–8:11).

Scripture interpreters partial to ancient rabbinic thought point to the dual commandments voiced by Jesus as the two imperatives from which all other commandments derive. Such a view misses the point of Jesus' declaration. Jesus joined the two commandments together and made them one. As one, they form the "great" commandment — the only one that *must* be obeyed.

Keep in mind that Jesus discussed the great commandment in response to a specific question that prescribed the parameters of his answer. Speaking within the givens imposed by the questioner, Jesus identified the most important commandment in the Old Testament. This was neither his last nor his best word on either commandments or love. That came later. Toward the end of his public ministry, talking on his own initiative rather than in reaction to an inquiry from someone else, Jesus voiced a new commandment, which raised morality and love to a level never before anticipated.

The New Commandment

"A new commandment I give to you, that you love one another; even as I have loved you, that you also love one another."

(John 13:34)

Just after sharing the loaf and cup of the Last Supper with his disciples, Jesus made a statement that drove moral judges out of business. At least, it should have. With the force of tornadic winds, the words of Jesus swept away law-based behavior and reduced courts of self-righteous judgments to rubble. Jesus referred to his statement as a "new commandment," but it was unlike any other commandment that had ever been given. It was a "law" that completely freed Christianity from the tyranny of law.

The setting of Jesus' statement gives it meaning beyond what is obvious, which is enough in itself. By way of both disturbing words and dramatic actions, Jesus informed his disciples that he was about to die. Amid the mixture of shock, grief, and perhaps a modicum of fear that the disciples experienced as Jesus' news about what was about to happen started to sink in, they began to wonder about the specifics of following Jesus in the face of such an unexpected crisis. Surely Jesus did not expect them to follow him in death. So, how were they to live?

Jesus answered that question with a new commandment — "love one another; even as I have loved you" (John 13:34). Disciples of Jesus follow Jesus and keep the spirit of Jesus alive by loving one another. Indeed, love for one another is the distinguishing mark of the Christian community.

Self-love could no longer serve as the model for neighbor-love. Jesus challenged his followers to love other people as he had loved them. The new mandate from Jesus swept away all claims of privileges, rights, and merits so much a part of self-love, and replaced them with the impulse to relate to every person with a selfless love that finds expression in acts of grace. No one had to wonder about the nature of such love. It is a love that motivates a perfect individual to lay down his life on behalf of (for the good of) imperfect people who do not always appear even to appreciate such sacrificial love.

The new commandment redefines God-pleasing behavior. No longer is a person's obedience to traditional legal prohibitions the true measure of righteousness. Not doing wrong gives way to doing good as the essential characteristic of the people of God.[30]

What qualifies as "doing good"? How can we determine "loving" behavior? Look at Jesus, the criterion by which to measure all action. Doing good is doing what Jesus did — lifting up the fallen, reconciling enemies, forgiving sinners. Practicing love involves being patient and understanding, not giving up on anyone, and doing whatever has to be done (even to the extent of laying down one's life) to bring redemption to people, all of whom have done wrong and need redemption, but some of whom may not be aware of their need.

Apply the new commandment from Jesus to individuals who commit the old sin of adultery. Important insights appear immediately. People guilty of adultery should receive mercy. God does not write them off or give up on them in any way, and neither should any other person, especially a person seeking to be obedient to God. Placing blame, assigning guilt, and doling out punishment for any wrongdoing have to take a backseat (if they are allowed in the car at all) for people who comply with the new commandment from Jesus. Grace-full love is up front, an aggressive love that treats adulterers (and all other sinners) with grace.

The eleventh commandment, the new mandate that Jesus spelled out to his disciples somewhere in Jerusalem, sums up, if not overshadows, the Ten Commandments delivered to Moses atop Mount Sinai. Implicit in Jesus' admonition about practicing Christlike love was the warning that a person could keep the Ten Commandments perfectly (at least in theory) and still not practice the righteousness of a real Christian. Authentic Christianity trades in love and mercy.

A close look at the fundamental commandments recorded in the Bible confirms the assumption that law cannot answer the forgiveness question about adultery. Even the explicit prohibition against adultery in the Decalogue takes on new meaning when studied in its social context, compared with the new commandment stated by Jesus, and set amid the entire sweep of redemptive history described in the Scriptures.

Still a hunch remains — God deals with adulterers as with all other

30. Arthur John Gossip, "The Gospel According to St. John," in *The Interpreter's Bible*, vol. 8, ed. George Arthur Buttrick (Nashville: Abingdon Press, 1952), 693.

sinners: redemptively. As for the sin itself, the teachings of Jesus suggest that withholding love and grace from an adulterer displeases God as much as, if not more than, the immorality of adultery.

Law fails to answer our question about the fate of adulterers. Examining moral-theological definitions of adultery-related behavior and studying expositions of pertinent biblical commandments provide helpful insights into the complexity of the question about adultery, adulterers, and forgiveness. Clearly, God opposes the sin of adultery, like any other sin. But a study of specific biblical texts that address the subject of adultery must precede offering any conclusion about God's treatment of adulterers. To that task we turn next.

Tough Truths in Biblical Texts

Flesh is a parable of the Spirit.

Sam Keen[1]

TO SAY THAT the Bible is tough on adultery is a gross understatement. Without exception, every Scripture text that addresses the subject of adultery brands it as a sin — a sin against other people and a sin against God. Adulterous behavior breaks a basic religious commandment and disregards (or intentionally disobeys) the revealed will of God.

Yes, the Bible speaks harshly about the evil of adultery. But is adultery forgivable? Or is adultery a different kind of sin, a sin so horrible that no one who commits it can ever live beyond it or be rid of guilt imposed by it? How does the Bible answer such inquiries? Does Holy Scripture identify adultery as an (or the) unforgivable sin?

Most people formulate their opinions about the Bible's teaching on adultery as a result of the method by which they study the Scriptures rather than by the actual content of specific biblical texts. Two different approaches to the Bible promise a discovery of the Bible's teaching about adultery and the possibility of forgiveness for adulterers. However, each of these alternatives to Bible study leads to a different conclusion.

One method of research involves an examination of each verse of Scripture in which the word "adultery" appears. Any good concordance

---

1. Sam Keen, *Hymns to an Unknown God: Awakening the Spirit in Everyday Life* (New York: Bantam Books, 1994), 173.

of the Bible cites every verse that contains the term "adultery." Conclusions about adultery can be formed on the basis of comments about this wrong found in each of these texts. This approach to biblical understanding devotes little or no attention to the context of a specific verse's treatment of adultery and thus looks at only part of the story.

A second approach to discovering the Bible's teaching about adultery focuses attention on every Scripture passage relevant to the subject of adultery, whether or not the term "adultery" actually appears in a text (the rest of the story). Behind this method of study stands a strong conviction that biblical truth is larger than any one biblical text can reflect alone. Devotees of this second approach to Bible study look at all the Scripture verses that address "adultery" specifically, but also consider the context of these verses as carefully as the verses themselves. Seekers of truth direct detailed attention both to the immediate setting of a passage within a particular section of the Scriptures and to the larger context of this passage, which involves the entire sweep of the biblical narrative.

Knowing up front that how we study the Bible's teaching on adultery dramatically affects what we conclude from that study, we must question whether or not differing perspectives on adultery derived from the different methods of study can be reconciled. The best way to answer that question is to sample each method of study and then work with the results.

Before demonstrating each of the two basic approaches to a study of the Scriptures, let me confess that I am going to hedge a bit— especially on the first method of investigation, which virtually disregards the context of a verse. I will try to determine a verse's pronouncement on adultery by considering only that verse — separated from, in isolation from, any other biblical text. Having completed that task, however, I intend to place each text in its appropriate historical-biblical context to see if its setting confirms the more restricted study or throws new light on it.

PART OF THE STORY

In addition to various legal declarations regarding adultery scattered throughout the Bible, three verses of Scripture address adultery specifically and unambiguously. Each of these biblical texts condemns adultery with such forcefulness that neither divine nor human forgiveness for the sin seems very likely. At least, it looks that way at first glance. Each of these biblical texts merits careful study.

Society and Adultery: "Kill the Scoundrels"

> If a man commits adultery with the wife of his neighbor, both the adulterer and the adulteress shall be put to death.
>
> (Leviticus 20:10)

Ancient Israel endowed its laws with religious meanings not found in the legal requirements of other Near Eastern cultures. Israelite leaders considered every law an expression of God's will. Subsequently, they interpreted any legal violation as rebellion against God. Religionists insisted on a strict administration of the punishment appropriate for every illegal action. Israelites believed that if the community failed to punish all who broke the law, God would punish the community.[2] Thus, in Israel — only in Israel — people judged the moral offense of adultery punishable by death.

Associating crime and punishment is understandable — break a law and you must pay for it. Correlating the nature of a person's punishment with the severity of that person's crime makes sense. But why establish capital punishment as the penalty appropriate for the sin of adultery? Isn't that a little unbalanced? A study of the seventh commandment in the Decalogue reveals how early Israelites regarded adultery as primarily a female crime. Even on those rare occasions when males were assigned guilt for this sin, no one looked at adultery as an indication of moral depravity. Why, then, the death penalty for adultery?

The severity with which Israel responded to adultery developed more out of an interest in purifying the nation than from a desire to punish adulterers. Israel felt called by God to be a "holy" people, a nation distinctly separated from all others. For this reason, Israel sought to purge itself of all wrongdoers, to rid itself of evil people. Without question, the death penalty provided a quick and effective means of doing away with unwanted individuals.

In a sense, the practice of capital punishment in ancient Israel

2. Moshe Greenberg, "Crimes and Punishments," in *The Interpreter's Dictionary of the Bible,* vol. 2, ed. George Arthur Buttrick (Nashville: Abingdon Press, 1962), 734.

corresponds to the practice of excommunication in the new Israel, the Christian church. Early Christian communities banished from their fellowships persons guilty of certain sins, relegating them to life outside the covenant community.[3]

The Levitical prohibition of adultery, which assigns the death penalty to all who disobey it, seems straightforward enough — adultery is wrong; adulterers will be killed. However, further study reveals that qualifiers, extenuating circumstances, and other conditions affecting the law's application rapidly crept into significance.

For example, when an act of adultery took place in the open country, only the man was judged guilty. Legalists reasoned that the man must have forced sexual intercourse on the woman, who was devoid of anyone to whom she could appeal for help. On the other hand, when adulterous behavior took place in a city, legalists charged both the man and the woman with sin. In a populated area where a woman could have asked for help if she had wanted it, so the presumption went, she must have consented to sexual intercourse (Deut. 22:23-27). In the first instance, authorities executed only the man. In the second instance, both the man and the woman were killed.

The official administration of Leviticus 20:10 was not nearly so absolute as the stark prohibition of the text suggests. In fact, dramatic imbalance characterized applications of the commandment. Responsibility for initiating legal proceedings to charge a man and woman with adultery fell to the offended husband. However, the law made no provision for a betrayed wife to press charges against her adulterous husband and call for the punishment of him and his lover.

Eventually rabbis modified the Mosaic code to give more protection to women. The Talmud declared that a woman could not be convicted of adultery unless proof could be established that the woman in question knew the law on adultery. As a result, convicting an adulteress became practically impossible. Even in this situation, however, a husband maintained the right to divorce a woman charged with adultery but not convicted of the sin.[4]

So, what do we learn from this Old Testament commandment in

3. Nathaniel Micklem, "The Book of Leviticus," in *The Interpreter's Bible*, vol. 2, ed. George Arthur Buttrick (Nashville: Abingdon Press, 1953), 101-2.

4. "Adultery," in *The Jewish Encyclopedia*, vol. 1, ed. Isidore Singer (New York: Funk and Wagnalls Co., 1956), 217.

the Levitical code? Without question, this law condemns adultery and prescribes the worst possible punishment for participants in adulterous behavior. However, exceptions dotted the application of this law and inequity characterized the law's designated punishment for violators.

Other important insights into the nature and use of this piece of Levitical legislation arise out of an examination of its cultural and biblical contexts. Israel, like many of the cultures surrounding it, approved of polygamous marriages as well as monogamous marriages. Also, Israelite morality allowed a man to enjoy sexual relations with a concubine or with a slave apart from either the charge or guilt of adultery. Culturally, then, the Levitical mandate against adultery permitted extramarital relationships (for men) that by almost any definition qualify as adultery.[5]

The Scripture verses immediately surrounding Leviticus 20:10 detail several other acts of immorality that the nation must judge. From the perspective of the Old Testament as a whole, adultery stood as only one of twenty-three different offenses for which laws prescribed the death penalty. Other capital crimes included possessing and serving other gods, practicing magic, cursing (or blaspheming) God by words or deeds, working instead of resting and worshiping on the Sabbath, owning an ox that gored another person to death, having sexual intercourse during a woman's menstrual period, striking a parent, and becoming involved in various types of homicide.[6]

So, again the question: What is to be learned from the prohibition of adultery in the Levitical code? Succinctly stated, Leviticus 20:10 declares that adultery is wrong — a breach of the moral law and a sin against God — and that adulterers should be killed. That's it. That is all the text actually says. However, looking at the larger picture of which this text is only one part provides additional insights, which contribute to a correct understanding of the text.

Persons who point to the severe punishment for adultery prescribed by this ancient text to argue for a debilitating, unforgiving treatment of adulterers today had best recognize the flimsy nature of their reasoning and its dramatic inconsistency with Christianity. Churches that appeal to this Old Testament law to justify excommunicating adulterers from their fellowships must be asked if they respond with equal severity to

5. W. Gunther Plaut, "Genesis, Exodus, Numbers, Deuteronomy," in *The Torah: A Modern Commentary* (New York: Union of American Hebrew Congregations, 1981), 558.

6. Greenberg, 738.

people who don't observe a day of rest and worship or to individuals who practice a contemporary form of idolatry. Yes, the law labeled adultery a serious sin — no more serious, though, than violating the Sabbath principle and bringing dishonor to God by other forms of ungodly behavior.

Shockingly, this Leviticus text indicates no interest in redemption, a concern always present in the ministry of Jesus and his followers. Contrary to the push to guarantee a morally pure fellowship around him, Jesus spent most of his time associating with notorious wrongdoers. Obviously, Jesus did not consider protecting his reputation nearly so important as offering redemption to all who needed it. When confronted by people about to enforce the Levitical penalty assigned to adulterers, Jesus refused to single out adultery as a special sin and sent all would-be executioners away to repent of their own sins.

God and Adultery: "Unrequited Judgment"

> Let marriage be held in honor among all, and let the marriage bed be
> undefiled; for God will judge the immoral and adulterous.
>
> (Hebrews 13:4)

Included in a collection of diverse moral admonitions appended to the New Testament letter called Hebrews, this brief verse purposed to affirm marriage rather than warn against adultery. However, the author of the text makes clear that God judges adulterous behavior.

The writer of Hebrews linked adultery with fornication. Both taint creation by abusing the divine intention for sexuality. But the two are not synonymous. Adultery breaks a marriage vow. Fornication involves more general sexual promiscuity.

Most likely, the writer included this verse in Hebrews as a defense of the moral legitimacy of marriage. Ascetics (perhaps like those in the Qumran community) commonly rejected marriage as an inferior moral state, a concession to the desires of the flesh. The admonition "let the marriage bed be kept undefiled" was a decorous way of affirming that "intercourse is untainted,"[7] sexual intercourse within a marriage is morally all right.

7. Louis H. Evans, Jr., *Hebrews,* Communicator's Commentary, vol. 10 (Waco, TX: Word Books, 1985), 243.

From the point of view of Levitical purity, "undefiled" meant "those who have wives live as though they did not" (see 1 Cor. 7:29).[8] Only a celibate life could qualify as morally responsible for persons who judged every act of sexual intercourse to be evil (see Lev. 15:16-18). This is not the Hebrew meaning of the phrase, however. The Hebrews text warns against sexual promiscuity among both the married and the unmarried (not judging sexual intercourse as inherently evil).

The brief statement in Hebrews concludes with the words "God will judge fornicators and adulterers." No surprise here. God judges everybody. God judges all behavior — good and bad. Did the writer intend this phrase on judgment as a simple observation ("God judges our behavior") or as a stern warning ("God will get people for such behavior")? Obviously, we don't know.

God's judgment takes many forms. Often people use "the judgment of God" as a label with which to describe the natural consequences of an immoral act. Negative consequences stemming from evil actions do represent judgment. But it is not a vindictive judgment intended to bring harm to each evildoer. Rather, such judgment exists within the acts themselves (certain consequences inhere in certain kinds of behavior).

In a real sense, God's judgment simply confirms the way things are. Adulterous behavior breeds lies, betrayal, hurt, anxieties, fear, and countless other actions and emotions that erode meaning and joy in life. God does not cause these negative consequences. Adultery does; or more accurately, adulterers bring these consequences upon themselves. God only confirms the sequence of an act and the consequences which that act sets in motion.

Two aspects of judgment become important in understanding the significance of this text. First, judgment is God's business, not ours. Only God possesses the qualifications to pass moral judgments on other people. Second, God's judgment exists as a dimension of God's love, not as a contradiction to or a negation of God's love. The loving God uses even judgment in the cause of redemption.

Robert Jewett views this entire section of Hebrews as a call to "shared vulnerability."[9] This noted New Testament scholar recognizes

---

8. George Wesley Buchanan, *Hebrews,* Anchor Bible, vol. 36 (Garden City, NY: Doubleday, 1983), 231.

9. Robert Jewett, *Letter to Pilgrims: A Commentary on the Epistle to the Hebrews* (New York: Pilgrim Press, 1981), 230.

that risks come with the territory in communal life. Weaknesses emerge and mistakes occur. But neither weakness nor error is an occasion for condemnation so much as a credential for ministry. Living by faith requires viewing life in the light that emanates from the "city that is to come" (Heb. 13:14). As Jewett observes, "It is to live without final answers, to keep the channels of communication open," and to make decisions fully realizing that we will never produce a "lasting city" or "entirely eliminate the threats that make *faith* necessary."[10]

So, what does this singular reference to adultery in the epistle of Hebrews contribute to our understanding of adultery? Not a lot, really, but what is there is very important. First, adultery is wrong. The text suggests no question about that truth. Marriage, which merits honor and fidelity, suffers from adultery. Second, God judges adultery like all other forms of immorality — such as not demonstrating mutual love, neglecting to offer hospitality to strangers, failing to remember prisoners, loving money, and chasing after strange teachings (see Heb. 13:2-9).

Three truths implicit in this verse equal its explicit comments in importance. God judges adultery; that's explicit. The first implied truth is the corollary reality that God alone can make such judgments. Judging other people's moral character lies beyond our ability or responsibility. Second, God's judgment is sure. But readers who look elsewhere understand that the purpose of God's judgment coincides with the intention of God in both creation and redemption — merciful love. Third, moral people relate to each other in all circumstances (whether at the height of moral achievement or in the depths of moral failure) under the influence of the love of God. We are to avoid adultery while loving and offering to help adulterers.

Adulterers and the Kingdom of God: "No Entry"

> Do you not know that the unrighteous will not inherit the kingdom of God? Do not be deceived; neither the immoral, nor idolaters, nor adulterers, nor sexual perverts.
>
> (1 Corinthians 6:9)

What a frightening statement! Does adultery disqualify a person for citizenship under the reign of God? Read alone, these two sentences in

10. Jewett, 232.

1 Corinthians indicate as much. This declaration from the apostle Paul stands along an adulterer's pilgrimage like a huge billboard declaring "No Hope" and like a barrier at the threshold of the kingdom of God warning "No Entrance."

Does Paul's assertion represent a major change in God's revelation about the basis of fellowship with God? In the apostle's other writings, as in the four Gospels, faith alone stood as the prerequisite to reconciliation with God and acceptance by God. Has answering a question about adultery (Did you or did you not commit adultery?) usurped the centrality of expressing faith as the primary determinant of a person's relationship with God? If that is the case and a whole new view of salvation is constructed on the foundation of this one text, far more than adultery is involved. Anyone guilty of *any* kind of immorality will be prohibited from entering the kingdom of God ("the unrighteous will not inherit the kingdom of God"). What's going on in this passage?

In this letter to a troubled community of Christians in Corinth, Paul contrasts what the Corinthian Christians once were with what they had become in relation to Christ. He writes to a church filled with individuals guilty of the wrongs he enumerates — sexual sins and property sins that hurt other people and harm one's own mind. Paul emphasizes the fact that Christ frees people from any lingering guilt imposed by their past sins and gives them a new life with God.

But what are we to make of this business about adulterers being denied entrance to the kingdom of God? No person who has committed adultery can alter that fact regardless of the intensity of a desire to do so. So, if adulterous behavior assures automatic rejection from participation in God's reign, nothing can be done about it. Nothing! There goes hope.

Yet this whole passage in Corinthians is about change and hope. Paul's most crucial point underscores the transforming power of God's forgiveness. People who have committed adultery and experienced God's forgiveness enter the kingdom of God not as adulterers but as forgiven children of God who have committed adultery.

God does not allow the guilt of a sin to define a person. Through grace-full forgiveness, God removes the stigma of every potentially defining sin (adultery-adulterer, untruth-liar) so that people can live as the children of God. Persons who brand other individuals according to the sins in their lives violate the intention of God, who offers grace and forgiveness to all.[11]

---

11. In this volume I have referred to people guilty of adultery — both males

Paul writes to the Corinthians to indicate that an incessant continuation of immorality does not reflect the reality of redemption (see also Matt. 13:41-43; 25:41-46). Where redemption occurs, life changes. Sin still happens, perhaps even adultery. However, it is not a lifestyle but a cause for sorrow, penitence, and a new experience of forgiveness.

To be sure, sexual promiscuity often creates moral confusion. Persons caught up in an adulterous relationship experience great difficulty distinguishing between egoism and unselfish concern, love and duty, sexual passion and the life of the Spirit, if they even try to exercise such discretion. But this situation does not lie beyond the reach of God's grace or exist outside God's interest in forgiveness. To conclude that any sin excludes a person from fellowship with God represents a "heathenish" perspective on God.[12] Similarly, an attempt "to reduce sexual ethics to a precise moral code is antithetic to the biblical faith."[13]

THE REST OF THE STORY

A study of individual Scripture texts in isolation from the broad context of biblical truth can be as misleading as it is depressing. Readers toy with a conclusion of "no hope" while examining a God-inspired book of hope. However, individual passages of Scripture tell only part of the biblical story (and like any partial truth can achieve the status of heresy if carelessly emphasized too enthusiastically). The rest of the story emerges through an engagement with the larger message of the Bible.

---

and females — as adulterers. Because of my conviction that *being* should not be defined by *doing,* I have struggled with the appropriateness of this term. I have chosen to refer to people who have committed adultery as adulterers in no sense to define their character by their behavior but only to indicate their participation in this sin and to prevent a repetition of the lengthy phrase "a person who has committed adultery."

12. Otto A. Piper, *The Biblical View of Sex and Marriage* (New York: Charles Scribner's Sons, 1960), 206.

13. William Baird, *The Corinthian Church: A Biblical Approach to Urban Culture* (Nashville: Abingdon Press, 1964), 85.

Everybody Is Guilty

> You that forbid adultery, do you commit adultery?
>
> (Romans 2:22)

"Not me!" a protest rings out. "I've never been unfaithful to my spouse in any way. Not only have I not committed adultery, I'm not guilty of any other sin as severe as adultery." Really?

Jesus understood adultery as an internal condition as well as an external action. Indeed, his whole approach to morality centered more on intentions and motivations than on words and actions. Jesus assigned primary importance to a person's spirit.

Legalists surrounded Jesus with moral judgments solely based on public behavior. They considered an action wrong because it violated a law that defined that particular action as wrong. Jesus rarely disputed the conclusion of legalists. Never did he defend an immoral action. Repeatedly, however, Jesus broadened the basis of judgment and clarified the nature of morality so that individuals standing in judgment or condemning another person for an immoral act could see their own complicity in evil, often in the same kind of immorality they were condemning.

More than once Jesus described the nature of a moral life while indicating the substance of immorality. Public appearances and social judgments made no contribution to his conclusions. On the subject of adultery specifically, Jesus acknowledged that "adultery in the heart can accompany outward hypercorrectness" just as "purity of heart can accompany acts that are outwardly dubious and condemned by society."[14]

The first major interpreter of Jesus, Paul of Tarsus, applied the Messiah's broader understanding of morality to a spirit of self-righteousness among some of his readers. In the midst of a diatribe against hypocrites, Paul asked, "You who say that one must not commit adultery, do you commit adultery?" (Rom. 2:22). The implied answer was "Yes, you do." The apostle challenged persons castigating individuals for breaking the legal prohibition against adultery while themselves violating the moral prohibition sounded by Jesus. Both Jesus and Paul realized people's tendency to condemn others for actions of which they, too, are guilty.

---

14. Eduard Schweizer, *The Good News According to Matthew*, trans. David E. Green (Atlanta: John Knox Press, 1975), 122.

Not only did Jesus redefine the nature of adultery, he positioned it on a continuum of evil that reveals its severity in relation to other acts of wrongdoing. Using a form similar to a contemporary Hellenistic catalog of sins, Jesus itemized acts representative of immorality (Matt. 15:19; Mark 7:21-23). Right alongside the sin of adultery, Jesus positioned jealousy, pride, and envy as expressions of immorality.

Jesus viewed self-righteousness as an indication of immorality every bit as serious as that of an act of disobedience to religious law. Without question, adultery is wrong in the teachings of Jesus; but so are envy, slander, jealousy, and pride.

Ironically, adulterers often fall victim to persons who embody the very attitudes Jesus set alongside adultery in his warning. "I have been tempted many times as you were," a man boasts to a colleague caught in an adulterous affair, "but I always had the moral strength to resist it. You could have done that too." Jesus saw little distinction between the immorality of the act condemned and the immorality of the attitude behind the condemnation.

Who has not committed adultery as Jesus defined this sin? If any declare themselves innocent, then let them be asked about their guilt in relation to pride (a deadly sin, one of the seven deadliest), slander (a kind of gossip akin to murder), or envy (a manner of looking at another's happiness or success with a desire to cast a spell on it)? And what of self-righteousness? Is anybody completely innocent?

Paul made the general observation "All have sinned." His conclusion squares with the teachings of Jesus, which define adultery and its equally immoral kin in a manner that makes everybody guilty. Everybody!

Salvation Is for Sinners

God shows . . . love for us in that while we were yet sinners Christ died for us.

(Romans 5:8)

Facing up to the guilt that besets all persons would be too much to bear were it not for the realization that the very sin that causes grief also qualifies us for the salvation that brings joy. Lostness is a prerequisite to being found; sinfulness is a precondition for forgiveness. It's not that anybody must try to fail morally in order to know Christ's redemption; everybody's got failure down pat already.

Critics of Jesus completely missed his point about unconditional grace. Wanting to limit the promise of salvation to people who deserved it, they encouraged Jesus to associate only with people known to be righteous. The critics' attitude evoked a stern response from Jesus, a reprimand wrapped in an instructive analogy — "Those who are well have no need of a physician, but those who are sick" (Mark 2:17). Ill people do not have to get well as a prerequisite to receiving treatment from a doctor. Likewise, sinners do not have to get their lives in order before Jesus will pay any attention to them. Jesus could not have stated the truth more clearly: "I came not to call the righteous, but sinners" (Mark 2:17). Sin qualifies a person as a candidate for salvation.

The "old-time religion" established a cause-and-consequence system of punishment and salvation.[15] According to the law, a sinner could escape punishment and experience salvation only through stringent individual efforts, correcting wrongs and proving merit for acceptance. Jesus shattered this self-help religion by introducing grace — what Paul calls "overflowing grace" (Rom. 6:23). A relationship with God replaced obedience to the law as the basis of salvation. To establish a new order, God stepped between the cause and the consequence of traditional religion and offered grace as a response to sin. God rejected the idea of quid pro quo relationships, addressing with grace the very sin that, by all rights, should invite punishment.

Nowhere is the grand initiative of God's grace more self-evident than in what is probably the best-known Scripture verse. Note the polar realities at the center of John 3:16 — the God of love on one hand and a world not interested in the things of God on the other hand.[16] A hostility toward God rightly deserving of punishment from God receives instead the precious gift of God's Son, who embodies the promise of salvation. No merit. No request. No logic. Just grace. God reaches out to the perishing with love and extends the possibility of salvation.

The chasm that existed between God and the world finds its closest counterpart in the gulf that separates sin and grace. No bridge can span the rift that stretches from sin to grace.[17] People who choose to live

15. C. H. Dodd, *The Epistle of Paul to the Romans,* Moffatt New Testament Commentary (London: Hodder and Stoughton, 1932), 99.

16. Leon Morris, *The Gospel According to John,* New International Commentary on the New Testament (Grand Rapids: Eerdmans, 1971), 128.

17. Karl Barth, *The Epistle to the Romans* (New York: Oxford University Press, 1977), 228.

under sin can do no better for themselves than rank sins according to their severity and draw up lists of prescriptions for righteousness, qualifications for receiving love, and prerequisites for redemption. They can't get to grace.

Grace comes only as a gift. But grace does come — to everybody, to all sinners. God unexpectedly builds the bridge. In the midst of sin, we discover love. Neither our love nor our goodness prompts God's love. As the apostle Paul understood, "God shows . . . love for us in that while we were yet sinners Christ died for us" (Rom. 5:8). Maybe that declaration does not convey the truth strongly enough. Not only were we sinners when God began to show love to us, we were actually "enemies" of God (Rom. 5:10).

The worst aspect of our lives places us in a position to experience the best aspect of life. All of us are guilty of something — if not adultery then something equally bad. However, our guilt qualifies us as recipients of God's forgiveness. God offers salvation not as a response to our good behavior but as a reaction to our need. Salvation is by grace.

Grace Makes No Exceptions

> Therefore just as one man's trespass led to condemnation for all, so one man's act of righteousness leads to justification and life for all.
>
> (Romans 5:18)

Law refuses to concede to the sovereignty of grace without a monumental struggle. Even people convinced that salvation comes by grace want to hang on to a little bit of law — not sell out completely to grace, but retain law as a helpful corrective lest grace become too radical.

Some folks prize grace at the entrance way to salvation before turning quickly to law as the guide, judge, and executioner (if needed) for the saved. In this scenario, a person reconciled to God by grace must prove the authenticity of his salvation by a life that conforms to the law. Though saved by grace, we must live in obedience to the law or receive punishment.

Other people continue to laud grace generally while refusing to apply it in certain specific situations. Developing their own lists of sins that preclude grace, these individuals make a mockery of the unconditional grace of God. "Conditional" is not an adjective that can accompany grace, because the noun destroys the modifier or vice versa.

God's protest against the wrongs of the world takes the form of grace.[18] God sees sin and responds with grace, all the grace needed to deal with the sin (Rom. 5:20). So abundant is God's grace that "grace abounds no matter what we do about our 'sins.' We can't make it abound any more than it does, either by committing sins or by not committing them."[19]

The opposite of sin is not moral perfection but faith — faith in the grace that takes sin away.[20] Likewise, the essence of obedience to the law is not moral success but love (Rom. 13:8), love that finds expression in grace. For Jesus, Paul, and us, the principle of all moral action is God's kind of love, a love indistinguishable from grace.

"But are there exceptions to grace?" The question is a crucial one. Does any sin — such as adultery — stand beyond the reach of love and defy the power of grace to forgive? No, absolutely not. "The last rule of the life of grace is that nothing can separate you from it."[21]

Numerous episodes in the ministry of Jesus demonstrate the inclusiveness of grace and the power of loving forgiveness. None, though, brings together quite so comprehensively all the major truths in "the rest of the story" about grace as the encounter between Jesus and the woman charged with the sin of adultery.

In this tense situation, Jesus challenged the self-righteousness of the woman's accusers (and would-be executioners). Without condoning the woman's sin or challenging the validity of the law's condemnation of this sin, Jesus requested that only people "without sin" (John 8:7) punish this adulterer. His words meant innocence. His point was that no one is without sin. Everyone is guilty.

However, the woman's guilt did not preclude God's forgiveness. Jesus rejected sin as a barrier to salvation, recognizing sin as an indication of the need for salvation. Refusing to behave as a judge, Jesus lived out his identity as savior. Nowhere is salvation more needed and more available than among sinners.

No exceptions! Grace is for everybody, even a woman "caught in adultery" (John 8:3). Jesus sensitively treated with grace an individual

---

18. Barth, 492.

19. Robert Farrar Capon, *The Mystery of Christ . . . and Why We Don't Get It* (Grand Rapids: Eerdmans, 1993), 172.

20. Capon, 171.

21. Robert Farrar Capon, *Between Noon and Three: A Parable of Romance, Law, and the Outrage of Grace* (San Francisco: Harper & Row, 1982), 177.

embarrassingly apprehended in the very act of adultery. In the face of a sin that could have been punished by death, Jesus provided the gift of life.[22]

CONCLUSION

No doubt about it, the Bible condemns adultery as a grievous sin. With equal clarity, though, the Bible commends grace as a way for sinners — all sinners — to experience new life. While individual biblical texts convey tough commentaries on adultery, other singular passages eloquently herald the magnanimity of grace.

Setting aside an examination of isolated texts and studying the truth inherent in the whole sweep of the Scriptures results in a realization of the universality of sin, the indomitable possibility of God's forgiveness, and the persistent pursuit of sinners by a tireless, fearless, unconditional, outrageous grace.

22. For more on the story of Jesus and the woman caught in adultery, see pp. 152-55 below.

The Answer: Grace

"Heaven would show mercy . . . hadst thou but the strength to take advantage of it."

Hester Prynne, *The Scarlet Letter*[1]

AS WE HAVE seen, although the Bible clearly considers adultery a sin, to the question "Is adultery an unforgivable sin?" the Bible shouts an emphatic negative. To the question "Can adulterers be forgiven?" the Bible trumpets a resounding positive. Both answers spring from the reality of God's grace. In fact, God's grace serves as the foundation on which all reactions to adultery are to be constructed.

WATCH OUT FOR LEGALISM

Religious law has a place — indeed, plays an important role — in the development of moral sensitivity. Christianity retains a solid appreciation for the contributions of Old Testament law to personal and social ethics. At the same time, those who know the law best readily acknowledge its inadequacy to resolve moral dilemmas with the compassion called for by Christ. Not all legal definitions of morality even agree with each other, let alone offer assistance to individuals struggling with issues of right and wrong. Worst of all, a preoccupation

1. Nathaniel Hawthorne, *The Scarlet Letter* (New York: New American Library, 1959), 187.

121

with law often hinders the work of redemption — the major concern of Christ.

Law can dictate a certain form of behavior, but law cannot determine the morality of that behavior. Many people abstain from certain actions prohibited by religious law, not because of a belief in the validity of the law, but because of a fear of the consequences of involvement in the forbidden actions. A wife of ten years never becomes sexually involved with a next-door neighbor to whom she is romantically attracted, but at every opportunity she socially promotes a bonding kind of emotional intercourse with him and privately nurtures a variety of sexual fantasies involving the man and herself. This wife keeps the law prohibiting adultery and loudly criticizes anyone identified as a violator of this law. However, she fails to practice the morality of fidelity.

The importance of law can be appreciated without being overestimated. At its best, law encourages no more than a minimal morality — a morality heavy with prohibitions encouraging various forms of abstinence — in contrast with the maximum morality commended by Christ — a morality laced with love, prolific with affirmations, and committed to the development of abundant life. Ethicist George Thomas captured the truth succinctly: "Moral law has an *important* but *subordinate* place in the Christian life; and its value lies in the fact that it *counsels us with respect to what love demands of us.*"[2] Love is the only absolute.

Affirmation and appreciation directed toward the law cannot be equally applied to the abuse of the law known as legalism. Moral and religious laws have the potential to aid the development of a responsible ethical lifestyle. Not so legalism. Legalists tend to harm the cause of morality every bit as much as do those people who disregard the law completely.

Nit-picking Casuistry

Legalists develop a nit-picking casuistry that misses the whole point of Christian morality. Almost invariably, people fascinated with law (in either theory or practice) explore the limits to which a law can be pushed without being broken. They seem much more concerned with how much

2. George F. Thomas, *Christian Ethics and Moral Philosophy* (New York: Charles Scribner's Sons, 1955), 137.

a person can get away with behaviorally without breaking the law than with encouraging the highest good a person can do.

Recently I recommended a friend of mine as a potential employee for another of my friends. Immediately the business owner raised questions about the accuracy of several rumors that had circulated charging the candidate for employment with adultery. I told the executive that my friend had been involved in some relational problems and explained that I did not know the nature of the relationships. "Did he have sexual intercourse with anyone other than his wife?" the employer pressed. I said, "Obviously, I don't really know the answer to that question. All I can tell you is that my beleaguered friend told me he did not become sexually involved with anyone outside his marriage." "Good," the executive exclaimed with a sigh of relief. "If he didn't have sex with someone else, that's all that counts."

I was pleased by the prospect of my unemployed friend getting a job. But I was disturbed by the rigidly legalistic morality I encountered in my other friend. If adultery means sexual intercourse between two married people who are not married to each other, then adultery can be avoided as long as coitus has not occurred. The fact that two lovers have engaged in a variety of sexual exploration and even brought each other to the point of orgasm does not matter. As long as a man's genitals have not penetrated a woman's genitals, these two people have kept the commandment against adultery regardless of the nature of their relationship and their involvement in other activities.

What kind of morality is that? Legalistic, of course. In the first place, a person should not be denied employment because he is guilty of adultery. However, if "no adultery" is a criterion for employment, how is that moral demand served by employing a person who has been involved in numerous extramarital relationships abounding in sexual interaction, though always stopping short of vaginal penetration? Legalists appear to appreciate persons who claim a technical innocence of adultery more than individuals who penitently confess adulterous behavior. What a devious casuistry! What a truncated morality!

Legalists tend to take more interest in assessing and assigning blame to people in trouble than in offering them help. It's in their blood. Guilty people must be punished. Innocent people must be protected. If one person bears more responsibility for an adulterous act than another, then the more aggressive partner must be identified. Facts are important, but if facts are not quickly forthcoming, perceptions will work just as well. You know what they say, "Perception is reality."

Driven by a boisterously confessed passion for truth (often difficult to distinguish from an expression of basic prurient interests), legalistic investigators jump through all kinds of moral hoops to determine who did what when. For what reason? To assign blame. Not only that, they also want to find out which of the two people involved in an adulterous act should carry the most blame for what happened. Why? To help or to hurt? To serve the cause of good for everybody involved or to satisfy an enflamed interest in condemnation on the part of a legalist? Take a guess.

Finger Pointing

Legalists have finger pointing down to a not-so-fine art. When a court of law serves as the dominant religious image in a person's life, that individual likely considers leveling judgments or passing verdicts on the behavior of others to be a form of moral piety. A legalistic mentality seems to elevate its holder to an exalted position in God's judiciary.

Strange, though — even legalists decide which laws to hold as inviolable and which laws to ignore. Stranger still, they always seem to appreciate most the laws that are furthest removed from mercy. For example, more than once Jesus stated emphatically, "Judge not" (Matt. 7:1; Luke 6:37, 41-42; James 4:12). This statement from Jesus carries all the weight of a commandment; even its form differs minimally from other "Thou shalt not's" and "Thou shalt's." The mandate is easily understood — don't pass moral judgments on other people. Yet, in their rush to arrive at moral justice, religious legalists daily hand out more judgments than come from the Supreme Court at the end of a term.

Only God possesses the wisdom required to pass judgment on the moral makeup of a person generally or on the morality of a specific aspect of a person's behavior. When individuals usurp this right, which belongs to God alone, everybody stands to get hurt. A judgmental attitude blinds people to their own sins and leaves them merciless in relation to the sins of others. Such an attitude also constructs barriers between individuals and inflicts hurts on social relationships. The end is not good.

Guaranteed Punishment

Once legalists find a person guilty of a moral error (and that is not difficult to do), only rarely can they be restrained from meting out the punishment they deem appropriate. They function as judge, jury, and executioner, to say nothing of posing as God. As long as a legalist is alive and the possibility exists that someone might not be punished for a sin, watch out. That legalist will not rest until a proper punishment for the guilty individual has been handed out.

The twisted consciences of legalistic moralists eventually deaden their sensitivity to true righteousness. Jesus endorsed a form of love-based goodness in which laws serve people, not vice versa ("the Sabbath was made for man, not man for the Sabbath" — Mark 2:27). For Jesus, a commandment either facilitated loving, redemptive behavior or lost its status as a law. Never, never did Jesus allow a law to stand in the way of redemption.

Jesus came down very hard on a group of people using an old law concerning tithing to avoid offering financial assistance to their needy parents. Behind the anger of Jesus stood a moral principle of continuing importance. To appeal to the law as a justification for not helping a person in trouble is a sin every bit as bad as, if not worse than, whatever wrong was done by the person left with no help.

In direct contradiction to Jesus' view of the redemptive purpose of law, wide-eyed, overly zealous crusaders for righteousness attack adulterers with a viciousness that makes the evil of infidelity pale before it. By some convoluted form of logic, these militant moralists reason that the more harshly they treat an adulterer, the more impressive will be their commitment to moral purity. Evaluated by such a distorted rationale, even the morally perfect life of Jesus would be suspect.

Moral laws can be helpful. However, legalism is seldom, if ever, beneficial. Jesus appreciated the law, but Jesus was not a legalist. Far from it.

Jesus Was Not a Legalist

Not only did Jesus react negatively to legalism, he avoided the identity of a new lawgiver, a latter-day Moses. To attribute legal status to the teachings of Jesus is to seriously misunderstand both the nature of Jesus and the morality he commended. Jesus made no effort to provide a moral code to which his disciples had to turn in every act of ethical decision making. Rather, Jesus laid down general principles of counsel, which elaborated the absolute mandate to live by love — the kind of love with which God loves all people.

Compassionate discussions of adultery and redemptive reactions to adulterers often have been sidetracked by legalistically inclined people trying to transform a comment from Jesus into cosmic law. Seeking to address the trivialization of marriage by religionists ready to grant an immediate divorce for almost any reason, Jesus spoke against divorce. The finality and bluntness of Jesus' words caused later interpreters to soften the impact of his prohibition by making adultery an exception to the rule, a justification for divorce. That revision has proven extremely costly.

Since one of the Gospel accounts uses the revised form of Jesus' statement, many interpreters of the Bible point to this declaration as an indication that Jesus leveled the ultimate condemnation at adultery, designating it as an unforgivable act. Others take this same statement from Jesus as a mandate for divorce among marital partners affected by adultery. Jesus intended neither of these understandings.

Jesus did not articulate a law against adultery, a law against forgiving people guilty of adultery, or a law requiring divorce in marriages hurt by adultery. Certainly Jesus wanted to preserve the sanctity and permanence of a marital relationship. However, never did Jesus elevate an institution (marriage) or a law (the prohibition against adultery) over a person. Nor did Jesus respond to sexual sins as forms of evil beyond forgiveness. Jesus consistently demonstrated God's love for sinners and called on all who follow him to allow that same kind of love to govern their lives.

A LIFE OF GRACE

Grace results from living by God's kind of love. Efforts to express God-inspired love amid the complexities, problems, and tragedies of people's moral dilemmas prompt a demonstration of grace. If you just have to have a law, that's it: live by grace. To obey God and to follow Jesus require a grace-full life.

Grace answers questions about adultery, just as it answers inquiries about other sins as well. Is adultery forgivable? Yes; definitely, yes. God responds to sin with grace. And so do the people of God.

Defining Grace

"Grace" may come across as a religious term understandable only to trained theologians. Such a concept of grace must be avoided. This book is not an academic treatise on grace but an explanation of how God responds to people guilty of adultery.

Once grace answers the question "Can adultery be forgiven?" other questions demand a response — questions like "How should the church behave in relation to adulterers?" Neither a classroom nor a worship center provides the primary environment in which people seek answers to these inquiries. Grace-related questions must be answered amid a shouting match in which a betrayed spouse lashes out at her unfaithful husband; in an anger-dominated board room where an employer wrestles with a decision about terminating an employee charged with marital infidelity; around a breakfast room table where, after reading the local newspaper's nasty charges against one of their friends, a shocked and disappointed couple discuss whether they will write him off or reach out to him. Any definition of grace that cannot withstand the tension and heat of these situations offers little help. Yet grace needs definition.[3]

Actually, crisis-fraught settings form the best backdrop against which to define grace in an understandable manner. Strictly intellectual discussions of grace conducted in sterile settings hardly ever get to the real, radical substance of the subject. Besides, grace usually surfaces amid a mess — a tragic set of circumstances, a barrage of charges and countercharges, a rapidly worsening situation in which people are about to multiply hurt.

Most simply stated, grace means taking the initiative to help someone who doesn't deserve it, someone who may not even request help. To act with grace involves relating to people not on the basis of what they deserve but in response to what they need. Individuals motivated by grace wade into morally murky, obviously problematic situations that they could easily ignore in an effort to lift out of a life-threatening quagmire of evil people who never should have been there in the first place.

Living by Grace

Living by grace, which means responding to persons grace-fully, requires overcoming natural tendencies to the contrary: accepting people we

---

3. For a collection of different definitions of grace, see C. Welton Gaddy, *Where Do You Go to Give Up? Building a Community of Grace* (Macon, GA: Smyth & Helwys Publishing, 1993), 73-74.

would like to run out of town; seeking to understand individuals whom we would prefer to shoot; attempting to help people we are not sure we like and whose behavior we despise. Embodying grace involves responding to evil with good; treating arrogant lawbreakers with sensitive compassion; and working like crazy to stop a bad situation from getting worse, when washing our hands of the whole matter would be the easiest thing to do and perfectly understandable.

Living by grace invites criticism. Grace never seems smart. Or wise. Grace is almost always controversial. Rarely is it politically expedient. Invariably grace-filled actions become the target of hurtful criticisms. Not uncommonly grace appears to shortcircuit justice. Some people even argue that grace undercuts righteousness. Hardly ever does a recipient of grace appear to be worth what grace costs the one who extends it.

Grace tolerates no ifs, ands, or buts appended to it. In fact, grace recognizes no exceptions at all. Real grace, the product of God's love, is unconditional. Help with strings attached is not grace.

Measured by contemporary standards and conventional wisdom, grace looks to be foolishness at best and a terrible weakness at worst. Acts of grace highly offend persons committed to fairness and justice. As people in the first century viewed the cross of Jesus as a scandal (*skandalon*), so people today consider acts of grace a scandal — much more of a scandal, in fact, than the sin of adultery.

Grace sounds too good to be true. But it is true. You can count on it. Unfortunately, the gospel itself sometimes sounds like wishful thinking. Thanks be to God, though, its truth is there for the asking, and the living.

Please do not misunderstand. Grace is more than an ideal, a doctrine, or a hope. Grace takes on flesh and blood in all kinds of persons. Specific situations define the nature of the work grace performs.

Adultery evokes predictable responses from grace and inspires detailable actions on the part of people of grace. To these challenging works of grace we now turn.

PART III

SCANDAL OF SCANDALS

Cecil and Nancy

Maybe . . . evil is where we meet God.

Robert Farrar Capon[1]

"CECIL WILSON! What a terrific surprise," an astonished Chuck Pullen exclaimed. Though he hated trite phrases and worked hard to express himself with precision, the unexpected presence of Cecil Wilson in his office reduced Chuck Pullen to a cliche. "You're a sight for sore eyes. What on earth are you doing here?"

No two people could have been closer friends. Chuck and Cecil met in a seminary classroom in San Francisco on the first day of orientation. From that moment to the graduation ceremony that placed a diploma in each man's hand, Cecil and Chuck had been inseparable. They studied together, ate together, and relaxed together. More importantly, they talked together, sharing doubts, hopes, convictions, dreams, anxieties — everything.

During the second year of his theological studies, Cecil met a young woman in San Francisco and fell head over heels in love with her. Seven months later, Chuck officiated at their wedding ceremony and joyfully pronounced Cecil and Nancy "husband and wife." Subsequently, Chuck became as good a friend to the couple as he had been to Cecil when he was single.

---

1. Robert Farrar Capon, *Health, Money, and Love . . . and Why We Don't Enjoy Them* (Grand Rapids: Eerdmans, 1990), 2.

"I really need to talk to you if you have time." Cecil's voice betrayed restrained emotions and conveyed an obvious need.

"You know I have time," Chuck responded, opening the door that led from a reception area into his office. "Come on in."

"Nice," Cecil observed as he looked around at the plush furnishings surrounding Chuck's desk. "You've done well. I'm really pleased for you."

"Tell me what's going on," Chuck interrupted. "I want to know why you're here, how Nancy is doing, if you have children, all that kind of stuff."

After graduation day at the seminary, the two close friends had moved in different directions. Chuck took a position as chaplain in a social work agency in southern California. Cecil moved to a small pastorate in the Midwest. Letters and phone calls between the two became less and less frequent. Chuck invited Cecil and Nancy to his wedding, but they were unable to attend. The last contact between the two had occurred almost five years before, when Chuck notified Cecil that he was moving to Tennessee to become the senior minister of a large downtown church in Nashville.

Cecil began to unfold his story as he made himself comfortable in a high-back chair. "I'm here because I'm passing through Nashville on my way to a new job in Virginia. Nancy is well, probably better than she has been for several years. We have two children, one in elementary school and one in junior high. They're great kids. One excels in the classroom and the other on the baseball field."

"I'm so glad to hear that," Chuck responded with sincere delight.

"But it hasn't been that way long," Cecil quickly added, his eyes dropping to stare at the carpet. "That's why I'm here. That's what I want to talk about."

In the silence that followed, Cecil braced himself as he looked to see if ascendancy as a big church pastor had altered the warm compassion of Chuck's earlier years. Not a word was spoken. Chuck looked at Cecil with openness and a desire for understanding.

"Five years ago I met a woman who turned my life upside down," Cecil continued. "I was not looking for a relationship, I don't think. My marriage with Nancy was good. We loved each other and fulfilled each other's needs. At least, I think we did."

Cecil risked another glance at Chuck. Still no sign of disapproval or threat of a forthcoming lecture.

"I met this woman in my work as a pastoral consultant with a family services agency. We became good friends while planning a project together. Over lunches and after evening meetings we discovered that we shared an amazing number of mutual interests, dreams, and beliefs. Our friendship deepened. Then romantic love developed — one of the most wonderful feelings I've ever known.

"Missy — that's what I called her — was married also. Both of us knew we were teetering on the verge of a volatile situation. You know what romance does to a person, though. We cast caution to the wind and acted the stereotypical part of foolish lovers.

"Chuck, my spirit soared." Cecil's face brightened as he spoke. "Every dimension of the relationship with Missy was exciting, rewarding, fulfilling. I wanted to be with her every minute of every day."

"Did Nancy have any idea what was going on?" Chuck's first question. And a fair one.

"Not for a long time. The demands of my work gave me plenty of excuses to be in touch with Missy by phone, whether I was in town or away on a business trip. Our shared responsibilities in the agency provided us with long expanses of uninterrupted time to spend together out of the office. Looking back on it, I'm sure some of our colleagues at work picked up on what was going on, but at the time we thought nobody had a clue.

"I don't want to bore you with the details of being found out, the hurt that ensued, and the dirty debris that piled up when Missy and I gave up on our relationship. I lost my job. Friends in our church turned against me and, for God-knows-what reason, didn't want to be around Nancy either.

"Thank God, Nancy stayed with me. Frankly, I don't know how she did it, but she did. I entered therapy alone and we began seeing a marriage counselor together. During the last two years our relationship has grown to new depths. I think we're better off than we've ever been, committed to a more honest relationship than we'd known before."

Cecil paused again to allow Chuck to express disappointment in him, condemnation, or whatever. Silence prevailed. The intense expression on Chuck's face communicated only compassion and an invitation for Cecil to continue talking as he willed.

"Now, here's what's really bothering me, Chuck. I don't know that you can understand, but I want you to try. The affair with Missy was wrong — evil, a sin, call it what you will. I knew our relationship was immoral at the time and I know it now. But it was a fabulous relationship. I loved Missy in a way I had never loved anybody else. I actually think I'm a better person because of that relationship."

"How so?" Chuck asked.

"I'm much more in touch with my feelings and less prone to handling every issue on the basis of detached reason. I can own up to my faults as well as to my strengths. I'm not afraid of risks. With Missy, I learned how to share both joy and sorrow, to weep and laugh. I discovered how to abandon selfishness."

"Quite a feat," Chuck remarked.

"Please understand me, Chuck, I don't ever want to have an affair again. The humiliation of discovery, the shame of deceit, the hurt I caused Nancy and the kids, the loss of work, the financial crunch — I don't ever want to have to go through that again. Yet, I think . . . no, I know . . . I'm a better person because of all that.

"My wife, our children, and I seem to be healthier and better adjusted today than we've ever been. Some really good things have happened as a result of that indescribably painful situation. Why, some days, I even think I may be more of an authentic Christian now than I've ever been."

"What's your question, Cecil?" Chuck asked, leaning forward, not pushing but gently probing.

"How can I still have warm feelings about Missy and speak positively about a relationship that nearly destroyed my family and wrecked my life? How can so much good come out of an immoral situation? Was I just lucky?"

Sensing that Cecil was not about to speak again right away, Chuck observed, "Some people would call it luck. I wouldn't."

The expression on Cecil's face was anxious and curious.

"I would call it grace," Chuck continued.

"Grace?"

"Yes, grace."

Cecil moved to the edge of the chair. "Do you mean to tell me that you believe an occasion of sin can serve as an opportunity for grace?"

"That is precisely what I mean," Chuck commented, beginning to smile.

"Good God!" Cecil said, without realizing what he was saying. After staring at Chuck incredulously for a full minute, Cecil buried his head in his hands and said it again, *"Good God!"*

Chuck walked over to Cecil's chair, placed a hand on Cecil's back, and whispered to himself, "You're so right, dear friend, you're so right. *Good* God."

The Gift of Grace:
Promise and Offense

The first and last word of the gospel is grace; grace as forgiveness and acceptance, grace as growth toward fulfillment and empowerment for new life.

James Nelson[1]

GOD'S GIFT of grace is more than some people can comprehend. Individuals religiously trained to think only in legal terms find the promises of grace too good to be true, more like flights of wishful thinking than solid assurances of theological reasoning. Troubled people plagued by a melanomic guilt long to believe in grace but suspect its reality since they have seen such sparse evidence of it in their community.

Like a child who has been offered a delicious piece of candy by a stranger, an adulterer ponders acceptance of grace with eagerness and hesitancy — desperately desirous to receive grace, but dreadfully fearful of what strings might be attached; amazed by the generosity of the giver, but alarmed that the candy-holder may be someone up to no good; wanting to reach out for the gift, but leery that someone might slap the extended hand; ready to abandon all inhibition and lay hold of grace displaying the joyful enthusiasm boiling deep inside, but nervously cautious because of previous disappointments and hurt.

Some people find grace downright offensive. Grace scrambles the

---

1. James B. Nelson, *Embodiment: An Approach to Sexuality and Christian Theology* (Minneapolis: Augsburg, 1978), 103.

logic that undergirds their judicious security and flip-flops values around which they have neatly arranged their lives: do good and all goes well, do evil and bad things happen; sin deserves to be punished and help should be offered only to those who help themselves; individuals must pay dearly for acts of immorality; and justice, not mercy, most responsibly conveys love. Such people fear consequences of grace that they have mistakenly conjured up in their minds — cheap forgiveness, a proliferation of sinfulness, no respect for law, chaos, a religion without demands. The predictability of law-based behavior provides a confidence and stability that forever resent the spontaneity and flexibility of grace.

Ironically, a cherished promise that inspires hope in one person offends another person because of its potential danger. An appreciated source of help for a troubled individual appears to a judgmental person as a threat to the moral foundations of society.

THE PROMISE OF GRACE

To understand grace is to take hope. At its heart is great promise. Folks who view grace as offensive base their conclusion on the very content of grace that incites such a riot of joy — a loving initiative to bring redemption to people who don't deserve it.

The News Is Always Good

Bad news has become so common that we suspect the credibility of good news. A form of Murphy's Law governs moral behavior — things will go as bad as possible; more likely than not, they will go worse than predicted. Given a choice between good and evil, most people aspire to good and choose evil every time. No reason exists to expect a bad situation to get better.

The gospel of Jesus Christ — announced by his message and embodied in his life — is good news, better news than anyone can anticipate. When introduced into a context of negative attitudes and pessimistic expectations, the gospel seems too good to be true, a pipe dream, wishful thinking in the mind of an out-of-touch idealist. The gospel's unwavering promise of grace strikes defeatists as scandalous, a stumbling block to viewing life with integrity.

Periodically people who claim to herald God's word hurt the impact of the gospel far more than help it. Offering a synthesis of cultural mores, personal opinions, and biblical truth under the rubric of the gospel, individuals yell at their listeners about fiery judgment rather than invite a reception of passionate grace. They take a lively message brimming with hope and make it sound like a warning cynically chuckled by a demonic representative from Hades.

Try as we might to change it, however, the Christian gospel resiliently resounds with good news. Not even the most tragic circumstances intimidate the gospel; not even the most vocal critics can silence it. The worse the situation that confronts the gospel, the better the gospel looks and the stronger is its promise.

So much for generalizations. Now for specifics. Here are several gospel themes that evoke gratitude and inspire hope.

The presence of sin in our lives does not sentence us to a hellish destiny. God looks at who we are as well as at what we do. At the very moment of our wrongdoing, God acts to save us from evil actions and enable us to live as good people. God refuses to imprison us within the narrow confines of our immorality. The gospel of God offers liberty, not captivity; forgiveness, not morals; grace, not condemnation.

Throughout history, God has claimed wicked people as potential saints and exercised the divine will through people whose moral resumés reflected little more than a recollection of misdeeds. Immorality does not determine destiny, not even when the sin is adultery. Destiny is a product of God's work, the God of grace.

Repentance is an experience of joy. Sometime in the distant past, somebody saddled repentance with a bad reputation. In the minds of many people, the very word "repentance" conjures up images of weak-kneed individuals groveling before a stern-faced judge, a guilty person desperately cajoling a distant deity to act with mercy. What a bad rap!

Repentance signals life taking a turn for the better. It is a change of direction that allows a person to move toward a new goal. Literally, the word we translate as "repentance" means to turn around, to reverse destinations.

A person who repents before God turns toward the epitome of love to face a future filled with grace. Through repentance, we move from frustration to fulfillment, from meaninglessness to purpose, from despair to hope. Pain may be involved in revisiting a source of guilt and sadness. However, the promise of repentance far outweighs the measure of pain involved. "Repentance is a flight to freedom, a human response to the R.S.V.P. of God's invitation to joy."[2]

God makes possible second, third, and fourth chances to correct mistakes and get on with life. Moral perfection does not accompany a confession of belief in the gospel. Followers of Christ continue to sin. The grace required to begin the Christian journey remains a necessity throughout that pilgrimage.

Jesus warned against limited forgiveness, conditional love, and restricted grace. He encouraged limitless compassion, excessive grace, and countless extensions of forgiveness. The gospel embraces no concept of a "three strikes and you're out" philosophy of life. Forgiveness can be found in a relationship with God and among God's people every time forgiveness is needed. We have multiple opportunities to turn our backs on the past and press forward — two, three, four times or more. Who's counting?

God reigns now. The promises of the gospel focus on the present, not just some distant future. The truth announced by Jesus at the advent of his ministry has not been rescinded: "The kingdom of God is at hand."

A few people always argue that the good news that is the gospel will not be realized until the conclusion of history. All their spirituality is futuristic — the good to be derived from God's reign resides in another realm, beyond this life. Nonsense!

Jesus embodied the grace he proclaimed. The possibilities of this grace fill every moment now. God's good news has not been placed on hold or delayed in any way. What the gospel offers, it offers in the present. Good news is here for the asking.

Nothing can separate us from God's love. Excited by a profound insight, the apostle Paul wrote of an assurance that provides unshakable security and sets our spirits soaring. "Nothing can separate us from the love of God." The tentmaker from Tarsus scribbled a rhetorical litany of would-be challengers to God's love — death, life, angels, principalities, things present, things to come, height, and depth. None of them can stop divine compassion — nothing "in all creation, will be able to separate us from the love of God in Christ Jesus our Lord" (Rom. 8:38).

Paul could have added immorality generally or adultery specifically to his list of ineffective barriers to God's love. No matter. Neither

2. C. Welton Gaddy, *Tuning the Heart: University Sermons* (Macon, GA: Mercer University Press, 1990), 29.

of these can separate a person from God's love any more than can height, depths, or death. Wrong acts do not frighten God away from a person who commits them. Lest Paul should be misunderstood in this text, elsewhere he wrote with equal clarity, "Christ died for us while we were still sinners."

Incredible but true, the gospel's promise of unqualified good news offends some people. Certain types of individuals thrive on bad news, laugh at the thought of a friend catching hell, delight in the dire consequences of an acquaintance's immoral actions. Judgment pervades this mind-set, which relishes punishment. You can see how the gospel appears scandalous to such people — a stumbling block to devotion to God. Too bad. Where the gospel prevails, the news is always good.

Acceptance for Everybody

Most fellowships among humankind establish membership requirements — enrollment fees, age ranges, academic credentials, and professional competence, to name a few. Similarly, some folks apply the principle of prerequisites to participation in the family of God. "You must be penitent, reverent, clean, pious, and sinless to be a part of our gospel fellowship." A virtually endless list of principles of exclusion unfolds. But it fails.

Just as "conditional" cannot stand as an adjective accompanying "love" (or "grace") that comes from God, "restricted" has no place as a modifier prior to a "fellowship" formed by the gospel of God. In both instances, the noun and the adjective disqualify each other. God loves everybody. And God's grace extends to all people.

To establish moral perfection as a prerequisite for receiving God's grace makes no more sense than positing good health as a requirement for anyone qualifying for medical care. God's grace is contingent on only one condition — a person's need for grace. God makes the one stipulation for receiving grace the one condition shared by every person in God's creation in need of grace.

No sin disqualifies a person from fellowship with God. Jesus entrusted the development of the church to people who betrayed him in his roughest hour — betrayed him after following him. Not even blatant infidelity stands beyond the reach of God's gracious capacity to provide forgiveness and fellowship.

When God throws a party, everyone is welcome. Guest lists are unnecessary. Everybody requesting entrance will be admitted. Jesus demonstrated the inclusiveness of God's fellowship through a series of delightful stories. In one, a son who spent himself immorally in a far country dined alongside a brother who sinfully resented his sibling's acceptance back home because their father loved and accepted them both. In another story, preparations for a dinner party patterned after "the Messianic banquet" included the host traveling to out-of-the-way places to invite to the meal people who had never been to a banquet (people whom some said *should* never attend a banquet).

Grace always attracts a motley crowd of people. Look at the individuals who cluster around grace. Almost to a person, they are failures of one kind or another — traitors, deserters, and the like. Without exception, they are sinners, every last one of them. However, for all these people, their evil is their ticket to the party, their wrong is the reason for their acceptance by grace.

The gospel promises acceptance. The entranceway to fellowship with God is wide open. All are welcome. Don't even think about trying to keep anybody out.

Justice for Nobody (Unless They Insist)

Justice represents law's best effort. But law's best cannot begin to measure up to the provisions of grace. To do justice means to give people what they deserve. To live by grace means to give people what they need, no questions asked.

Frankly, not everybody likes grace. Almost without exception, institutions resist it. Governments and religions in particular display a noticeable partiality for justice. Likewise, countless numbers of individuals prefer justice to grace. Advocates of a quid pro quo approach to life assert, "Tell people the rules. Give them a chance to obey. If they succeed, great. If they fail, hit them with penalties commensurate with the nature of their disobedience."

Raw justice holds out little hope for a better future, if the future gets considered at all. Enforcers of justice spend most of their time distributing rewards and enforcing punishments for people's past accomplishments and crimes respectively. Rewards typically get short shrift, though, because punishment demands so much attention.

From the point of view of justice, a respect for law demands punishment for all who break the law. How this punishment impacts an individual lawbreaker makes no difference. "She knew the rules, she broke them, and she has punishment coming to her," declares the logic of justice.

The gospel presents grave difficulties for hard-nosed (or is it hard-hearted?) legalists, religious or civil, who view grace as unfair. They question God's commitment to morality and suggest that God does a slipshod job of handing out judgments. Where grace prevails, people do not get what they deserve. Individuals who by all rights should incur incessant wrath and harsh punishment hear the gospel, meet God, find love, and walk away with hope.

Legalists reduce life to a moral equation: evil plus justice equals punishment (e + j = p). God skews the whole formula by substituting grace for justice and thus guaranteeing forgiveness (e + g = f). When the gospel has its way, love transcends law and salvation replaces condemnation for sinful persons.

God promises grace to everybody. Thus, nobody is restricted to the dealings of justice alone. However, if a person absolutely insists on living exclusively by the dictates of justice, God respects that desire while holding open an invitation to experience grace.

Forgiveness with No Ifs, Ands, or Buts

The gospel promises forgiveness to sinners. That's it. God offers forgiveness to all people — not forgiveness *if* or forgiveness *but*, just forgiveness.

Between people, conditions or qualifications often accompany offers of forgiveness. An executive says to an anxious employee, "I can forgive your failure if you will promise never to do such a thing again." Or a wife tells her humiliated husband, "I forgive you for your infidelity, but I don't ever want to see you again." That's not forgiveness!

Real forgiveness deals honestly with a person's sin. Then it works like crazy to bring about reconciliation and restoration in relation to whatever separation and destruction the sin has caused. Empowering a person to continue life after an evil episode is as much a part of forgiveness as enabling a person to confront a sin penitently and choose to move beyond it.

Even a person's profound grief over a former sin fails to guarantee the absence of any future sin. Forgiven people continue to sin and need forgiveness again and again. Thankfully, God does not withhold forgiveness from us until we can promise never to sin again. Were that the case, we would have no hope of dealing with our guilt. Jesus demonstrated the repetitive nature of divine forgiveness when he instructed his disciples to offer forgiveness to people as often as they needed forgiveness.

Assuring a person of forgiveness without assisting that person in the work of reconciliation and restoration is cheap. Saying "I forgive you" can be a religious-sounding means of washing one's hands of a guilty person in a bad situation without attempting to do anything to help. True forgiveness makes getting on with life easier, not more difficult, for the person (or persons) forgiven.

Failure as a Credential for Service

Grace turns society's evaluation of failure upside down. Ask almost anybody: personal failure jeopardizes an individual's future and even throws into question the person's worth. "Not so!" grace declares. "Failure evidences an individual's finitude. What's more, properly handled, failure breeds sensitivity to hurting people and creates a capacity for offering compassionate help."

In Nathaniel Hawthorne's classic tale of Hester Prynne, the author describes how this woman's badge of shame became a symbol of her ordination as a Sister of Mercy — "The scarlet letter had the effect of the cross on a nun's bosom."[3] Though initially her self-righteous neighbors condemned her, eventually people from all parts of the community sought Hester's counsel for their perplexities and sorrows. Recognizing Hester's journey through sorrow, people felt her sensitivity to and sympathy for their hidden wrongs.

Who knows the value of antidotes to hurt like a person who has been helped through a period of hurt? Who is better equipped to respond to the specific needs of a troubled person than an individual who has experienced victory over those same needs?

It's not a sure thing. Failure embitters some people. Occasionally a person uses failure as an excuse to withdraw into a shell. However, when failure meets grace and allows grace to do its redemptive work, the person who failed becomes grace-full and the failure becomes a credential for service.

Perceptions of perfection in others play poorly among individuals

3. Nathaniel Hawthorne, *The Scarlet Letter* (New York: New American Library, 1980), 57.

struggling to live past a major error in their lives. Hurting people do not want to get within a hundred miles of an individual who appears never to have experienced any pain. Conversely, troubled persons more readily request help or accept assistance from people who obviously understand their plights. Thus, a person's failure in the past often serves as a badge of authenticity, opening doors into the experiences of people traumatized by failure in the present and promising them help.

I know a man whose life plummeted from the lofty heights of professional success to a bottomless pit of emotional despair. An adulterous affair cost him his marriage, his job, his savings account, and, for a while, his will to live. Slowly, with the support of two staunch friends and guidance from a skilled therapist, his downward spiral stopped and the man began to get better. Eventually, healing came more rapidly and a renewed desire for life emerged. Today my friend functions with a level of personal fulfillment unlike any he had previously known. A quiet, genuine humility has rubbed out every trace of loud arrogance in his personality. Sensitivity to the troubles of other people has filled the vacuum formed by the departure of his self-centeredness. Responding to people in need provides him plenty of joy.

Not long ago, my friend confessed, "I've never been happier," as a prelude to the rhetorical question, "Why did I have to go through so much hell to learn the joy of helping other people?" Failure can be a powerful teacher. Combined with grace, it can provide a new lease on the future and empower a lifestyle of service.

Adultery does not negate the possibility of meaningful acts of service. An occasion of infidelity touched by grace can result in a renewed commitment to fidelity in marriage, faith, and ministry. Having known the hope-full benefits of grace amid the depths of pain in an immoral relationship, a recovering individual can resolve to serve as an instrument of grace and a herald of hope for others. Such an individual incarnates a realization of the Bible's promise that wounds possess the power to heal.

THE OFFENSE OF GRACE

Grace outright offends some people, usually people who have not yet experienced a real need for grace. Not always, though. Confusing strength in convictions with rank inflexibility, some folks want their religion strong and strict, unbending and unerring. Passionately devoted to law, these people consider grace an outrage to decency, a flaw in moral fidelity, an embarrassment to justice. Such folks would complain to God about the existence of grace were they not convinced that rules prohibit complaining to the Almighty about anything.

Religions that preach bootstrap theories of salvation ("grab your bootstraps and lift yourself out of the mire"), that view divine blessings as contingent upon individual merit, and that commend illusions of moral perfection find grace almost intolerable. People who find great joy in condemnation and take delight in meting out judgment can hardly stomach grace.

Consider grace's response to a few of the more popular charges leveled against it.

"We've got to have some standards."

Agreed. We have to recognize standards, respect and protect values. And we do. Unfortunately, grace is not always one of them.

Individuals who care more for standards than for persons had best be challenged to define the standards of interest to them. A system of values can inspire character development that leads to maturity and responsibility or can justify immaturity as the cherished status quo and irresponsibility under the guise of "being tough on sin." It all depends on the values involved. One approach to ethics nurtures compassionate spirituality and provides an outlet through which beliefs become helpful actions, while another breeds insensitive, passive dogmatism.

Standards provide security. But an infatuation with security can function as an enemy of authentic biblical morality. Witness what happened in the life of Jesus. Opponents of Jesus grew in number because his teachings jerked the rug out from under secure religionists by turning the fundamental values of Judaism upside down.

According to Jesus, motivation exceeds action in ethical importance; what transpires inside a person is more significant morally than what happens outside a person. Moreover, Jesus assigned more value to individuals than to institutions. Perhaps most revolutionary of all, and thus repulsive for many, was Jesus' insistence on the priority of grace over justice. Establishing the moral superiority of merciful love jeopardized traditional sources of security. You can't ever tell what kind of crazy thing love is likely to do.

Yes, we have to have standards. However, the nature of the standards that claim our allegiance is every bit as important as their existence.

Popular standards make God appear unfair.[4] To establish civil justice or social fairness as the norm by which sinners should be treated leaves God looking morally lax and frighteningly unjust.[5] Viewed from a legal perspective, Jesus functioned as a crazed iconoclast rather than as the beloved Messiah. Conscientious people committed to traditional moral values opposed the mercy-based ministry of the Son of God and finally crucified Jesus in the name of God.

Reverse the situation. Rather than judging God by popular standards extant in our society, take an honest look at individuals in light of God's standards. The ethics of God as revealed in the ministry of Jesus bring to a screeching halt those people pointing fingers of guilt at each other. We are all guilty, every last one of us. No one is free from immorality. According to the standards commended in God's word, everybody bears a measure of guilt even in the matter of adultery.

The ultimate standard in Christianity is compassionate mercy — grace — the quality that the author of the fourth Gospel used to describe the essence of Jesus.[6] To understand how grace functions as a moral standard, all we need to do is look at Jesus. Like Jesus, grace favors honesty, fidelity, and responsible stewardship. Like Jesus also, however, grace cares for people who fall short or fail completely in all these areas.

Some people consider grace an enemy of morality. "You grace-folks will let just about anything pass," they complain. No; they are wrong. "But that's not all," these folks continue. "There's not anybody you wouldn't try to help." Right; they've got it. Grace swiftly and decisively opposes immoral acts, unhampered by moral ambiguity. At the same time, grace responds to people involved in immorality with compassionate sensitivity and specific offers of help.

---

4. Robert Farrar Capon, *Health, Money, and Love . . . and Why We Don't Enjoy Them* (Grand Rapids: Eerdmans, 1990), 167.

5. John Jacob Raub, *Who Told You That You Were Naked? Freedom from Judgment, Guilt, and Fear of Punishment* (New York: Crossroad, 1993), 59.

6. The author of the fourth Gospel writes of Jesus, whom he refers to as "the Word became flesh": "From his fullness have we all received, grace upon grace" (John 1:16).

"Grace is foolish."

Judgments about grace hinge on perspective. If punishing an adulterer by making life more difficult for him and his family seems more reasonable than helping him deal with the evil of his sin and get on with the good of his life, then grace is foolish. Looked at from the point of view of redemption, however, grace makes good sense and appears totally sane.

The people of God cannot afford to write off every activity that society labels "foolish." Critical endeavors such as friendship, sensitivity, service, laughter, worship, and love qualify as irrational concerns in a success-driven, materially measured social order. But how could we live without such foolishness?

Critics of grace charge that people take advantage of grace and make those who live by grace look foolish. They're half right. Often, people in need do take advantage of grace. However, that reality signals a problem with the abusers of mercy, not a problem with the merciful.

Perhaps we're a bit too defensive about people labeling grace and practitioners of grace as foolish. So what if it is? So what if we are? The apostle Paul provides a profound insight into this situation — "God's foolishness is wiser than human wisdom" (1 Cor. 1:25), he wrote. The scholar from Tarsus readily understood why the world called God's people foolish: God's truth looks foolish to those who don't grasp it by faith. So he turned the tables on critics of the gospel. Paul took the term hurled at him by his peers as criticism and turned it into a word of commendation, even honor — "We are fools for Christ's sake" (1 Cor. 4:10).[7]

Grace is not foolish, but wise, practical, compassionate, helpful, Christlike, and godly. If conventional wisdom considers grace foolish, though, so be it. Biblical wisdom sees it differently.

"An assurance of grace discourages repentance."

This observation reflects a serious misunderstanding of both grace and repentance. People do not have to be browbeaten into reaching out for joy, which is the nature of repentance. In reality, a discouraged sinner

---

7. C. Welton Gaddy, *God's Clowns: Messengers of the Good News* (San Francisco: Harper & Row, 1990), 6-7.

wants nothing more. Grace simply undergirds an individual's movement toward repentance and rejoices greatly when it occurs.

One school of religious thought mistakenly prizes threats and warnings as precursors of repentance ("Repent or perish!"). People with this mind-set hold grace in reserve, anxious that it be distributed only as a reward for the penitent. However, grace refuses to wait until repentance has been confessed to go to work. Grace serves as effectively as a prelude to repentance as it does as a consequence of repentance. Acts of love lead far more people to genuine repentance than ever arrive there as a result of holy harangues.

How on earth would grace discourage repentance? A directly opposite reaction seems more likely. Assuring an adulterer of God's unceasing love and making her aware of God's people's desire for her life to take a turn for the better will cause a guilt-plagued woman to move quickly toward repentance (which means nothing less than doing an about-face, turning life around for the better). Grace functions as an incentive, not as a hindrance, to repentance.

Since grace eagerly leads its recipients into experiences of joy and encourages in them a resolve to live more abundantly, the path of grace passes straight through repentance. Grace sees no more need to avoid repentance than to become hung up on it. A person's genuine sorrow over wrongdoing brings a thrill to grace, but nothing like the thrill that grace enjoys when a person fully realizes the impact of God's (and other people's) loving forgiveness.

"People have to be accountable for their wrongdoing."

The Bible could not agree more. Take, for example, a statement in Romans: "So, then, each of us will be accountable to God" (14:12). God holds us accountable for our behavior. However, God refuses to allow our actions to diminish divine compassion — relating to us strictly in a tit-for-tat fashion; treating us precisely as we deserve to be treated; forcing on us an-eye-for-an-eye morality. Evidence of God's unwillingness to allow personal accountability to restrict grace also appears in Romans: "While we were enemies, we were reconciled to God" (5:10).

By definition, grace involves *unmerited* favor, initiatives for good in response to evil deeds. Aggressive acts of kindness directed toward and on behalf of a person who in no way deserves them form the substance of grace.

Behind anxiety about accountability for wrongdoing resides a person's fear that someone may get away with something, walk away from a sinful situation scot-free. Often the unspoken line that undergirds this concern reads, "I had to pay dearly for my sins and so should everybody else."

Grace does not destroy accountability. An individual guilty of adultery grapples with the consequences of that sin as long as he lives — rebuilding and nurturing trust with a betrayed spouse, admitting his capacity for relational promiscuity, guarding against exposure to temptations too strong for him to handle, feeling the scorn of certain acquaintances who can never forgive anybody for anything, and continuing therapy to assure emotional health. Plenty of adulterers continue to struggle with repercussions of their immoral behavior decades after an adulterous episode. Accountability is a necessity — "Yes, for whatever reason, I did it; I am responsible. I must accept the consequences of my sin and deal with them as positively as possible."

Grace can't eliminate all the bad repercussions of a sinful act any more than it can excuse accountability. Grace can, however, prevent a person from having to carry needless burdens and deal with negative situations that can be avoided.

God does not eliminate personal accountability in situations of immorality. However, God takes into the divine being consequences of evil that rightly belong to a sinner — not avoiding accountability but sharing it. That's grace. And that's how grace-full people act toward other people in trouble because of adultery or any other sin.

"Punishment is the best deterrent to wrongdoing."

At stake here is the dreadful assumption that fear influences behavior more powerfully than does love. Those who voice this opinion believe the threat of punishment inhibits bad decisions in a way unachievable by the promise of abundant life. Such thought takes the gospel of unmitigated good news and attempts to turn it into a bellicose warning about what's going to happen to people if they don't do right. That approach, in turn, lifts the burden of redemption out of the heart of God and squarely slams it down on the backs of people, who then must earn whatever salvation they want or need.

The origin of punishment resides in sin, not in God. All God has ever wanted for people is a good life. However, because God created persons as free moral agents — individuals willing and able to make moral decisions — a possibility of sin developed. Likewise, because of the nature of sin, the reality of punishment quickly fell into place. Sin contains within it the promise (or threat) of punishment. It's not so much something God does to sinners as something sinners do to themselves (ourselves).

God's greatest desire centers on saving people from every adversary — sin, punishment, the whole bit. God's business is deliverance — always has been, always will be. God's love finds expression in a persistent, generous summons to salvation, not in a trigger-happy propensity for punishment.

"Now, wait a minute," someone complains. "You're ignoring a whole lot of the biblical text. Passage after passage talks about punishment generally and hell specifically. God does more than offer salvation." That complaint is partly right and mostly wrong.

People who don't like good news and don't want anything to do with salvation see the gospel as bad news. Even then, the gospel is not really bad; it just looks bad to a person who is blind to good. Individuals bring punishment on themselves — infidelity brings on the misery of mistrust, dishonesty stirs discord, and adultery causes pain. None of those negatives, each of which appears as a punishment for the wrong that preceded it, can be blamed on God.

Some people would not be happy without the prospect of hell. So God obliges this sickly need and allows people to turn their backs on love and grace if they so choose. As C. S. Lewis pointed out long ago, though, the doors of hell are locked from the inside. Hell is the construction of people who just can't stand the thought of living with God. In Robert Farrar Capon's words, hell is a state "where unforgiving bastards are totally and eternally in charge of everything."[8] An unwillingness to forgive reigns in hell, "an eternal conviction that wrong should be prevented whenever possible and punished whenever not."[9]

Grace deems reconciliation a better approach to wrongdoers than damnation, love a stronger motivation for living than resentment, and help a greater source of hope than punishment.

"Grace encourages sin."

Across the years, reasonable explanations of grace have failed to silence this erroneous assumption about it. Indeed, the apostle Paul ran into

---

8. Robert Farrar Capon, *The Youngest Day: Shelter Island's Season in the Light of Grace* (San Francisco: Harper & Row, 1983), 81.

9. Capon, *The Youngest Day,* 80.

precisely this broadside against grace in his conversations with early, law-sensitive Christians. Critics of grace chided the missionary theologian, asking, "Are we to continue in sin that grace may abound?" (Rom. 6:1). In other words, "If responding to sinners with grace is such a big deal, if grace finds immense satisfaction in addressing sinners, surely we do grace a favor by continuing to sin. We give it work, provide grace an opportunity to really shine."

Such logic aroused indignation in Paul. How can anyone who knows the least bit about grace even imagine grace encouraging sin? "By no means!" the apostle roared (Rom. 6:2). Grace represents God's effort to usher people into life at its best. Sin makes no contribution to that effort. Just the opposite actually; sin messes up life, filling people's days with misery instead of birthing within them the joy that God intends.

Elation over the discovery of a remedy for a terminal illness does not spawn hopes for a rabid epidemic of the illness. Finding a therapy that softens the impact of relational hurt does not incite a desire to experience horrific hurt. The grace that brings hope to sinners never encourages sin.

Notwithstanding the fact that adultery is a sin against God, why on earth would anyone encourage an adulterous relationship just so the guilty parties can experience grace? Look at the fallout of adultery — shattered self-esteem, broken-hearted spouses, lost jobs, embittered social acquaintances, and battered reputations, to name a few. How could a sane person even insinuate that grace encourages that kind of pain, when grace works tirelessly to lessen the hurts in people's lives?

Some people wear blinders that prevent a recognition of the goodness of grace. Narrow-minded loyalty to law, a penchant for denunciatory judgment, a preoccupation with quick retaliation, or an insistence on punishment for every wrong hampers an ability to see the attractiveness of grace. Folks cannot celebrate God's gift of grace in the presence of sin for fear that someone might allow a fascination with the glory of grace to distract them from seeing the severity of sin.

"Forgiveness has its limits."

Says who? A lot of people, of course, but not the incarnation of grace. Jesus called for unlimited forgiveness, forgiveness every time forgiveness is needed.

Peter, a fiery first-century disciple of Jesus, questioned his leader about the appropriate number of times to forgive a person: "Lord, if my brother sins against me, how often should I forgive?" Peter wanted a law that defined the limits of forgiveness. This spiritual relative of all of us desired to do the right thing, but not to overdo it, not to offer more forgiveness than the law required.

Jesus answered the inquiry about how many times to forgive a person in a manner that made the question irrelevant. Forgiveness has no limits. Jesus told Peter that no number could be established as a guide to offering forgiveness. Grace-filled love extends forgiveness as often as people need to be forgiven.

"I could forgive her adultery once, but not twice," a man told me, talking about a friend. "That's too much. Anybody can make a mistake one time," he continued. "To repeat a sin, though, makes me think there is a pattern there — a reason for distrust, a cause for condemnation rather than forgiveness." Spiritual math differs from traditional methods of addition and subtraction, requiring an exercise of the heart rather than intellectual expertise.

Counting wrongs naturally leads to establishing limits of forgiveness when law is the primary means of measurement (seven times, or maybe seventy). Viewed from the perspective of grace, however, a similar tally of wrongs points forgiveness toward numbers that reach into infinity.

"Well, this is no way to run a world."

A last-ditch protest against grace argues that communities of humankind cannot operate under the authority of grace. "Things would begin to come apart amid the confusion," a critic argues. "Love might overrule justice, or well-deserved criticism might be silenced by sensitive understanding. Efforts at reconciliation would reduce our enemies to a ridiculously small number. Instinctive retaliation toward hurtful people would be halted by a passion for their redemption. Instead of punishing individuals who deserve it, we might end up praying for them. We just couldn't be sure of anything. We have to have law and justice to have order."

A strong case can be made against the wisdom of establishing grace as a fundamental guide in social actions. Grace is rarely, if ever, politically correct. It sides with the "wrong crowd" and challenges majorities that ruthlessly exercise power. Actions of grace — embracing lawbreakers and working to restore the lives of moral failures — offend high-minded individuals who insist on running a tight, legalistic ship. Grace sets people on edge as it upsets traditional values, affirming weakness and challenging strength, embracing losers and humbling winners.

Additionally, grace is forever ill-timed. Grace consistently fails to consult newscasts, public opinion polls, and national surveys in deciding when and how to express itself. Grace acts instinctively and spontaneously rather than at just the right moment to find social acceptance. To tell the truth, there is never a good time for grace. Somebody will always be offended by its inappropriateness and untimeliness as well as its openness and generosity.

Grace is risky, no doubt about it, a fact that frightens some people into denouncing its value for society. Grace does what is right without waiting for assurances that its recipients will respond in kind. As a result, individuals occasionally take advantage of grace, even abuse it. Undaunted by such behavior, however, grace insists that those who abuse it must not be allowed to terminate its usefulness for those who in receiving it find their lives restored and renewed.

Estimates of the worth of grace depend entirely on how one looks at things. If condemnation makes more sense than forgiveness, if punishment is more attractive than helpfulness, if hatred seems preferable to community, and if fighting the consequences of evil appears to make more sense than lovingly replacing evil with good, then grace fails as a standard by which to run the world. However, if comforting identification with hurting people, tireless efforts to facilitate help for individuals in trouble, restored relationships, lives turned around for the better, and the development of a society that prizes mercy appear desirable, then grace deserves a fair shake in the world.

To argue that endorsing the priority of grace is no way to run a world tips off listeners to the kind of world the speaker wants. Personally, I want something more than that: a community in which grace is a fundamental reality.

A PICTURE OF GRACE

A picture is worth a thousand words according to conventional wisdom. Thankfully, early Christians preserved an oral portrait that accurately depicts both the promise and the offense of grace. We almost did not get to see this picture, though.

A story of Jesus' encounter with an adulterous woman about to be killed by a self-righteous mob circulated in the early church. According to this fragment of history, in a bold and dramatic gesture, Jesus challenged a stirred-up group of men eager to enforce the law, which prescribed capital punishment for individuals guilty of adultery. Jesus neither denied the validity of the Old Testament prohibition against adultery nor condoned the woman's adulterous behavior. However, Jesus insisted on moral integrity, requesting that only people completely free from sin participate in the execution of this woman. When, in response to Jesus' words, not a single onlooker lifted a hand to do the woman harm, Jesus instructed the anxious woman to leave the scene of her judgment and begin a life devoid of adulterous behavior.

Though this intriguing narrative-portrait provided pungent insights into the grace-dominated character of Jesus, devotees of Jesus in the primitive community of faith were scared of it. Sexual promiscuity pervaded the pagan society that surrounded the early church. Christian leaders, who labored to make distinctions between disciples of Christ and other members of first-century society, feared that a portrait of Jesus demonstrating grace toward an adulterer would weaken prohibitions against this particular sin. They did not want this pericope included in the lectionary materials that they used in worship; it was not a part of the gospel that they wished to preserve.

Virtually no biblical scholar questions the authenticity of this controversial story. Research has traced its existence back to the second century. All the material in the narrative squares nicely with the nature of Jesus' ministry and person (though the manner in which the narrative develops is more consistent with the style of the Synoptic Gospels than with John). Yet no early manuscripts of the Gospels contain this story from the life of Jesus. The account appeared only in late texts of the Western church (sometimes after John 21:24, sometimes following Luke 21:38, and still again at the end of John 7:53, the spot where most people now place it). Eastern Christians did not preserve the narrative at all.

Because translators of the King James Version of the Bible worked with so many Latin manuscripts that contained the story of Jesus and the adulterous woman, their edition of the Bible included this episode from Jesus' life. Clearly, though, that was not the intention of the early Christian community. At least in the minds of some ancient Christian leaders, the story highlighted a teaching with dangerous implications. As

Augustine later explained, the church set this narrative of grace aside "to avoid scandal."

Amazing! Even in the primitive community of faith, grace appeared scandalous. The application of grace to a convicted sinner seemed risky. How little some things have changed.

Originally, the whole situation may have been a setup to entrap Jesus and get him in trouble with authorities. Jewish law clearly defined adultery as a capital offense.[10] A woman caught in the very act of adultery deserved to die. Those who stepped forth to kill her did no more than offer themselves as instruments of God's will. Conversely, Roman law, which did not prescribe such harsh reaction to an adulterer, prohibited killing a person for this offense. Enemies of Jesus, well aware of his reputation for merciful actions, intended to put him in a bind. Faced with a judgment about this guilty woman, Jesus would either offend Jewish authorities or anger Roman authorities; it was one or the other in the minds of his opponents. He would be in trouble regardless of the decision he made.

Surely Jesus must have resented these people reducing a woman to a thing to be manipulated for their own purposes, using a hurting human being like an inanimate pawn in a chess game. However, he stayed focused on the issue at hand. Skillfully avoiding the trap so cunningly set for him, Jesus turned the issue on his attackers.

Jesus immediately demonstrated the pity for which he was noted. Then he reiterated that judgment is not the prerogative of sinful humankind. As Jesus admonished the crowd to stone the woman if they were without sin, he used a word that meant not only "without sin" but also "without sinful desire." Jesus offered a straightforward challenge: kill this person guilty of adultery only if you have never desired to do or thought about doing what she did.

At no point did Jesus indicate the woman had not done anything wrong. He took her sin seriously. Adultery was (and is) a grave form of

---

10. Sometimes Jewish authorities punished adulterers by strangulation rather than stoning. The *Mishnah*, which consists of the codified law of Judaism, prescribes a detailed method for strangling adulterers: The man to be killed is made to stand up to his knees in dung. Executioners place "a soft towel set within a rough towel" around his neck "(in order that no mark may be made, for the punishment is God's punishment). Then one man draws in one direction and another in the other direction, until he is dead." William Barclay, *The Daily Study Bible: The Gospel of John*, vol. 2 (Philadelphia: Westminster Press, 1956), 2.

immorality. However, Jesus reacted more harshly to a mean-spirited condition of self-righteousness than to a physical act of evil. Jesus instructed the woman to go away and sin no more. In other words, Jesus let the woman know that this experience of adultery did not have to be the last word on the nature of her life. Without glibly saying, "Don't worry about it, what you did was no big deal," Jesus lovingly encouraged the woman to begin a better life. Ironic, isn't it, that the only person on the scene qualified to judge the woman chose to exercise grace rather than judgment?

What a dramatic picture of grace. Jesus' actions portray the fullness of its radical nature. Grace identifies with an adulterer and challenges as well as seeks to silence judgment directed toward that person. Grace opposes a moral authority that drives a sinner deeper into despair rather than seeks to lift a sinner from a bad situation and provide the person with a reason for hope. Grace shows pity on an adulterer; mercy is its instinctive reaction. Grace refuses to allow an episode of adultery to serve as the ultimate commentary on a person's character. Without in any way condoning the sin of adultery, grace seeks to halt negative reactions to an adulterer and create an opportunity for that person to enjoy a life that changes for the better.

"Oh, sure," a cynic quips, "you can paint a pretty picture of grace when someone else is involved. What if Jesus had been the one offended by this woman? How would he have reacted then?" Obviously those pertinent questions point to a hypothetical situation. Any answer would be purely theoretical. However, a real, historical situation parallels this old narrative and provides an answer to the cynic's basic inquiry. Jesus *was* victimized by infidelity. He experienced betrayal among the most intimate relationships of his personal life. Jesus hung dying on a cross because of the infidelity of people whom he loved. Anger would have been easy, resentment readily understandable, and bitterness highly appropriate. But Jesus' words to his executioners conveyed grace: "Father, forgive them."

The Corrective Work of Grace:
Responses to Adultery

God has no problem with losers.

Robert Farrar Capon[1]

ADULTERY EVOKES a variety of responses within society, affected families, and guilty individuals. Unfortunately the vast majority of these responses make a bad situation worse and increase the amount of pain that those involved must bear. That's wrong, a wrong in need of correction — correction inspired and shaped by grace.

Grace wades into adulterous situations eager to ease hurts, facilitate help, encourage forgiveness, and midwife reconciliations. However, sizable barriers block the path of grace, threatening to discourage its progress or halt it altogether. Often, then, before grace can make its most valuable contributions to a situation, extended time and intensive work must be devoted to corrective actions. Grace approaches spiritual and emotional wounds much as a physician treats a physical wound — the bleeding must be stopped before efforts to facilitate healing can begin.

Grace sets its agenda while taking a serious look at both society's reactions to an adulterer and an adulterer's reactions to herself. Grace deals first with what's wrong. Then, as quickly as possible, grace moves on to create what is right.

---

1. Robert Farrar Capon, *Health, Money, and Love . . . and Why We Don't Enjoy Them* (Grand Rapids: Eerdmans, 1990), 110.

SCATHING SOCIAL REACTIONS TO ADULTERY

Society has a love-hate relationship with adultery and adulterers. People flock to movies to drool over stories of heroes and heroines caught in adulterous relations. Scores of readers go through stacks of romance novels detailing extramarital erotica. Tell these same individuals about two people they know who have become partners in an adulterous relationship, however, and watch out for a severe response of righteous indignation mixed with moral outrage. For some reason, the revelation of a real affair prompts a sudden epidemic of abnormal piousness.

Not all people react to adulterers in such a harsh manner. Some folks do not even raise an eyebrow when learning of a friend's adulterous behavior. Unfortunately, their reaction stems from apathy concerning morality rather than from compassion or grace. Some people just don't care what others do as long as it doesn't affect them personally. This attitude also is problematic.

A few individuals always step forward to respond to adulterers with love and grace. Predictably, though, a proliferation of more vituperative reactions hinders their good efforts. Many folks respond to adulterers with the same extreme negativism that they direct toward adultery.

Blame Game

The attitude of a moral legalist is a wonder to behold (preferably from as far away as possible). Every situation of wrongdoing catapults a legalist into a search for truth about who should bear the blame for what has been done. Assigning blame seems to be mandatory, a far higher priority than planning ways to help.

The blame game rarely proceeds objectively. Certain factors cloud important judgments. For example, if a family member and a non–family member are charged with adultery, the family member tends to remain innocent until proven guilty while the non–family member looks guilty right away. ("He must have taken advantage of her. She would never have done such a thing unless she was misled or tricked. I know her.") Similarly, a neighbor is not as likely to be a target for blame as a person from the other side of town. ("She came in here and started flirting with him. I could just kill her for seducing him.") You see the way it works.

Objective or not, blame placing proceeds. Moral detectives unleash an outlandish barrage of interrogations. "Who made the first move toward an affair? Did one of you try to end the relationship? Who first expressed romantic feelings to the other? Did either of you resist the other's sexual advances?" If a clear delineation of guilt and innocence can be established, no one has to waste any help on the guilty party.

Evidence that blame may rest on the wrong person — that is, the person the blame placers thought innocent — often causes a rapid reassessment of the situation. "Well, she may be guilty, but her husband drove her right into that relationship. Bless her heart. I blame him." Or "He would never have become involved with that hussy had his situation at work not been so bad lately. That company just destroyed him."

What's the use? Why is blame placing so important? Why not take the time spent in discovering whom to blame for an affair and invest it in finding ways to help both affair participants get on with their lives?

Grace is not interested in blame; it's not disinterested either. Blame just doesn't matter much to grace because grace acts with compassion toward all in need, regardless of how little or how much blame for wrongdoing has been assigned to them. Blame may be a big deal for religion, a fascination for religionists interested in moral scorekeeping. Not for grace, though. Grace really doesn't have time for it. There's too much redemptive work to be done to spend time pointing accusatory fingers at people.

Lethal Labels

Here's where things begin to get really nasty — when name-calling starts. Common reactions to adulterers bring to mind branding season on a cattle ranch. A foul scent of searing hurt fills the air. Persons self-appointed to be in charge of everything shove white-hot branding irons against the reputations of individuals guilty of adultery. The sin of adulterers condemns them to life in a herd that bears a permanent brand indicative of evil. Range-riding moralists see to it.

Labeling an individual blurs the all-important distinction between what a person has done and who a person is. But, of course, that is the intent — to make an activity the sole determinant of an individual's identity. Refusing to recognize any complexity in an extramarital relationship, eager moral cowpokes quickly brand the people involved. Tragically, label wielders assure that an adulterous action becomes the sole definition of a person.

Applying these lethal labels is a Godlike act—determining people's futures, eradicating freedom, negating the possibility of change, stifling hope—with one major exception. God would never be part of such a life-defeating enterprise. God refuses to lock people into their pasts or to limit any individual's potential in the future. God's love makes short work of labels. Everybody is a person—not a cheater, a whore, a womanizer, a slut, a playboy, a bitch, a Casanova, a seductress, or an infidel, but a person.

Grace rejects labels outright, relating to every individual as a person created in the image of God. All that counts is everybody's potential to enjoy an open future. The contrast is striking: while a posse of moral range riders tries to herd adulterers together so they can sear them with a permanent brand, agents of grace open the doors of the corral and throw away all the branding irons.

"Schadenfreude"

The word *Schadenfreude* captures society's ambivalent reactions to adultery like no other. Unfortunately, the English language has no equivalent term. *Schadenfreude* is that pleasurable sensation that arises when hearing news about another person's misfortunes.

Joshua Halberstam, who introduced me to this intriguing word, describes *Schadenfreude* as the opposite of envy. "Envy is your private dejection at seeing another succeed; *Schadenfreude* is your private joy at seeing another fail."[2]

Most people respond to reports of someone else's infidelity with moral indignation, sympathy, and curious delight. Make that someone else a disliked competitor or a person whose success is envied and the pleasure prompted by the bad news increases significantly. A *Schadenfreude* approach to an adulterous situation causes an individual to say with a certain amount of sincerity, "I'm so sorry to hear that about them," and in the same breath, with an internal smile, to request, "Tell me all about it." Both the sincerity and the delight are real.

Schadenfreude gives justification to vicious gossip and to uninformed judgment. Consider the public's fascination with flashy news headlines about the failures of well-known individuals. The more detailed the

2. Joshua Halberstam, *Everyday Ethics: Inspired Solutions to Real-Life Dilemmas* (New York: Penguin Books, 1993), 6.

National Enquirer–type stories the better. People justify gossip by convincing themselves that they must know all about an adulterous situation to be informed enough to offer help to the adulterers. Maybe so. But such a fascination with the details of a sinful situation seems to feed a perverse delight more than to create a desire to offer assistance.

Most folks would be too embarrassed to come right out and say, "Well, I'm glad he finally got his comeuppance" or "I'm tickled to death that that pious witch wound up in bed with a total stranger." Count on it, though, such thoughts prevail, even among friends. The prevalence of *Schadenfreude* within society offers little promise for the betterment of the adulterers at whom it's directed.

Grace takes no delight in another person's wrong or pain. From the wisdom engendered by grace comes the sobering realization "That could be me. Like everyone else, I'm capable of such wrongdoing." From the compassion instilled by grace comes a driving desire to be redemptive. Grace cares little about what happened, why, or how, but only about how and when to help. Bending to weep with those who weep, grace has no time for snickering about people getting what they deserved. Its concern is how to make things better and get people what they need.

Angry Assassination

Anger and adultery go together. Adultery always incites anger, but the anger is not always rooted in righteousness or free from impurities. Selfishness regularly shows up — "He betrayed me. How could he not let me know what was going on? What about our friendship?" "Her actions cast a dark shadow over our business. We may lose customers." Disappointment also fuels the fires of anger — "I thought better of him." When a popular figure fails in marriage, people inevitably complain, "I set her on a pedestal. I guess you can't trust anybody." Though seldom acknowledged, even jealousy may contribute to an adultery-focused anger. A person may be mad at an adulterous friend for doing what he wanted to do but didn't.

Critics motivated by anger dump spirit-breaking loads of guilt on an adulterer. Then they rapidly move from criticizing the specific sin of adultery to terrorizing the adulterer with gross, destructive generalizations. Justifiable anger over a person's infidelity swiftly swells into an enraged denunciation of an individual personally. Moral opposition to adultery deteriorates into immoral attempts to assassinate the character of every adulterer.

Common charges leveled against adulterers run the gamut: "She never did have good judgment; don't trust her." "A man who can't be faithful to his wife is not responsible enough to deserve any measure of compassion." "He couldn't make a moral decision if he had a Bible in one hand and a prayer book in the other." "She has a basic character flaw and nothing can be done about it."

The morally indignant slink around like snakes in the grass, eager to attack adulterers and all who come close to them. In the aftermath of an adulterous relationship, slithering, venomous creatures bare their fangs and spurt their poison at an offended spouse to worsen her hurt, threaten her economic security, and prevent her from entertaining any idea of marital reconciliation; at a potential employer to kill the adulterer professionally; at a religious fellowship to guarantee a lack of the kind of support needed to survive a difficult situation; and at a news medium to assure the adulterer public embarrassment.

Not infrequently marital partners broadsided by adultery suffer almost as much in trying to heal wounds inflicted by a spiteful society's murderous attacks on their marriage as in trying to realize forgiveness and reestablish a covenant between themselves. Indeed, some marriages fail to survive an adulterous episode primarily because of the horrendous conditions imposed by people eager to strike a death blow at the guilty party.

Disturbing evidence and hurtful criticisms of their destructive actions do little to stop angry assassins' assault on adulterers. The infidel "asked for it," "deserves it," and "must be stopped," they explain.

Grace works to defuse irrational anger and to halt assaults on an adulterer's character. No deception or dishonesty is involved. Grace refuses to disguise a wrong as a right. However, grace advocates forgiveness and assistance, not punishment, as the proper response to a person trying to move beyond an immoral affair.

If people of grace cannot wrest the loaded gun from a would-be assassin, they often line up in front of and alongside an adulterer to form a wall of protection. Adultery no more relegates a person to the garbage heap of hopeless characters than honesty elevates an individual to the realm of righteous superiority.

The presence of grace within people creates an ache for life to be recovered, relationships restored, and possibilities for the future enhanced for everybody, adulterers included. Persons of grace channel all the power and influence at their disposal into concrete acts of support for hurting individuals and struggling couples.

Grace finds no joy in increasing a person's pain regardless of what the person has done. Grace rejoices when a person's pain — *any* person's pain — is alleviated. Like the One who incarnated grace most completely, people of grace find fulfillment in giving life to others, not in taking life away.

Rigid Righteousness

Sometimes righteousness looks for all the world like meanness. Indignant moralists can react to another person's sin in a manner that far exceeds in evil the despicable behavior of the targeted wrongdoer. Their judgmental reaction is worse than the immoral act that prompted it.

I know a couple who probably have been lost to the church forever. After an adulterous relationship rocked their marriage, church officials instructed both the guilty husband and his offended wife not to return to their local congregation until they were ready to stand before the membership to state their repentance and plead for forgiveness. What a barbaric demand. The inappropriateness of the officials' action becomes self-evident by placing that church's rigid requirement alongside the sweeping invitation from the open-armed Christ, "Come to me, all of you who are tired from carrying heavy loads, and I will give you rest" (Matt. 11:28). True righteousness pulsates with compassion and labors to lighten the loads people carry.

Rigid righteousness publicly decries the unrighteous, making no distinction between perceived immorality and the real thing. Suspecting a person of wrongdoing justifies a reaction equal to that evoked by an individual's confession of sin. Judgmental piousness baptizes rank gossip and pronounces it to be moral conversation. Individuals nervous about squeaky-clean reputations move far away from adulterers socially lest slight associations with the sinners stain their characters.

The New Testament describes the Pharisees as righteous people who went too far. A legitimate passion for moral responsibility among this religious group swelled into an illegitimate preoccupation with moral judgment. At their most extreme, the Pharisees made salvation contingent on an absence of sin. And look where it got them. Jesus directed some of his most severe words of criticism at this group. "You serpents, you brood of vipers," he said to them. "Woe to you . . . who shut the kingdom of heaven against men. . . . [Y]ou . . . have neglected the weightier matters of the law, justice and mercy and faith. . . . [Y]ou also outwardly appear righteous to men, but within you are full of hypocrisy and iniquity" (Matt. 23:1-39). What a scathing denunciation of rigid righteousness.

Grace has no part in this spiritual condition. In fact, grace feels much more at home among confessing sinners than among self-righteous, self-acclaimed saints. Grace naturally gravitates toward wrongdoers to offer acceptance and promise forgiveness. No groveling in guilt is required of guilty parties. No cajoling for compassion is necessary. No pleading for mercy is permitted. Grace rushes toward sinners to help them get on with living as quickly as it denounces the sins that bring hurt to their lives.

Hasty Punishment

In 1639 Mary Mendane was convicted of adultery and sentenced to be whipped. The judge also required her to wear an insignia on the left sleeve of her dress to publicize her guilt. Because of her failure to wear the insignia, officials burned her face with a hot iron.[3]

Rhode Island's early law prescribed swift and severe punishment for adulterers. The guilty party was "publicly set on the Gallows in the Day Time, with a Rope about his or her Neck, for the Space of One Hour." But that was not all. "On his or her Return from the Gallows to the Gaol, [the adulterer] shall be publicly whipped on his or her naked Back, not exceeding Thirty Stripes." Finally, punishment for adultery included a monetary payment of all court costs related to the prosecution of a person.[4] Other colonies simply expelled adulterers.

Things have changed over the intervening three hundred and fifty years, but not much. Society has altered its methods of punishing adulterers, though the swiftness and severity of punishment remain. Even expulsion remains an option. Note the institutions and organizations that dismiss employees charged with adulterous relations (if not formally, at least practically).

---

3. Sue M. Hall and Philip A. Hall, "Law and Adultery," in *Adultery in the United States: Close Encounters of the Sixth (or Seventh) Kind*, ed. Philip E. Lampe (Buffalo, NY: Prometheus Books, 1987), 70.

4. George Howard, *A History of Matrimonial Institutions*, vol. 2 (Chicago: University of Chicago Press, 1904), 173, cited in Philip E. Lampe, "Adultery and the Twenty-First Century," in Hall and Hall, eds., *Adultery in the United States*, 203.

Following an affair of several months, a counselee of mine confessed his infidelity to his wife. After a good deal of struggle and hurt, they agreed to stay together and work to make their marriage stronger. Tragically, a major hindrance to the rebuilding of their relationship came from the negativism of mutual friends. Virtually none of their long-term acquaintances supported the couple's efforts at reconciliation. Separation and divorce seemed a better, more appropriate option — fairer to her and just punishment for him.

In the aftermath of an adulterous relationship, a few people always hurriedly advise the offended spouse to terminate the marriage — "He doesn't deserve you anymore; leave him and make him pay for his bad judgment." Others rush to tell the guilty spouse she should follow through with her unfaithful intentions — "You wanted out; now go ahead, get out. See how it feels." Each bit of counsel signals punishment rather than help.

The cruelest, as well as most destructive, punishments leveled against an adulterer are those that jeopardize the well-being of an adulterer's family. A man came to my office in great distress and confusion because of sudden unemployment. His employer had dismissed him immediately after learning of his recent affair. Of course, the man was hurt (punished!). Far worse off, though, as a result of the employer's hasty action were the man's wife and two children. Already reeling because of her husband's betrayal, the sickly wife had to enter the job market in search of employment. Two innocent children found their educational development thwarted through no fault of their own. Whom did the employer punish?

In this instance, friends approached the adulterer's morally outraged former employer and pleaded for the guilty man's reemployment on behalf of his wife and children. No way. The employer scoffed at this request: "They're not my problem. He should have thought of what he was doing to his family before he started screwing around. Let him worry about his wife and kids." Not only were groceries in short supply and debts piling up in that household, but funds for much-needed marriage counseling were out of the question.

Explanations for such punishment escape me. Evidently some folks assume they strengthen their own moral values by punishing people who violate them. It's distorted logic, though very prevalent. People do not become more faithful to a particular moral standard by lashing out at everybody who breaks that standard. At most, those who inflict punishment may feel better. If that's the case, however, we are left to wonder what kind of ethic such a person follows anyway.

Grace has no time for calculating punishments commensurate with people's sins. It has better things to do. Grace tears down the scaffold to which the public brings an adulterer and from that spot urges would-be punishers to look at the cross of Christ before exacting punishment for a person's sexual sin.

The punishment of sin is God's business, if anybody's. And God is not interested. God recognizes the abundance of pain, the burden of guilt, and the agony of gnawing anxiety inherent in sin. So God enters a bad situation not to make it worse, but to offer assistance, encouragement, and hope to all the people involved in it.

Anybody can punish a sinner. It's easy to inflict hurt. Help requires more effort. Faced by a situation of infidelity, only a person filled with courage and compassion thinks and acts in terms of redemption rather than retribution.

Being mean to a sinner in Jesus' name is still being mean — and it's also misrepresenting the character of Jesus. God doesn't need moral crusaders clearing the landscape of all evil people (who would be left?) but harbingers of hope heralding the good news that God, not sin, has the last word about a person's life. Do people who cannot wait to punish an adulterer also eagerly pray as Jesus taught, "Forgive us . . . as we forgive"?

DETRIMENTAL PERSONAL REACTIONS TO ADULTERY

Adultery does not affect everyone the same way. Some people appear to shed adulterous experiences more easily than ridding themselves of a common cold. Not many, though. After an adulterous affair, most individuals spend the rest of their lives sorting through the emotional garbage they collected during the affair or while getting out of it.

No one else has to make sure adulterers hurt. Most of them take care of that for themselves. As if they didn't have enough pain to bear already, adulterers tend to impose more pain on themselves in the form of self-condemnation and regret. The difficulty of coping with this pain intensifies because typically the pain goes unshared. No longer available is the adulterer's former lover, who previously would have listened sympathetically to confessions of agony. An offended spouse does not particularly care to hear a betrayer's tales of woe. And friends are questionable as confidants. Often it is not until the pain borne in silent solitude reaches a critical level that an adulterer turns to a counselor and unloads the horrible hurt that has eroded life's meaning for too long.

Loss of Self-Worth

Disappointment in one's self commonly troubles adulterers. If a guilty person had harbored unrealistic self-expectations — "You'll never catch me in an adulterous affair!" — disappointment intensifies. Over time, unrelieved disappointment deteriorates into disgust or despair. A spirit of defeatism develops, and self-deprecation follows.

Healthy self-esteem disappears amid feelings of worthlessness. Audible hints of an adulterer's hurt often can be heard. A requiem for confidence and meaning plays like an endlessly recycling tape in the person's psyche: "I'm a failure. I'm not worth anything. I betrayed my spouse and proved I can't keep a promise. I violated my own moral code. Why would anyone trust me when I don't trust myself? I have nothing left to give others. No wonder no one wants to be around me, I don't want to be around myself."

Negative reactions from friends and acquaintances (like the reactions discussed in the previous section of this chapter) reinforce self-criticisms and confirm an adulterer's sense of worthlessness. Hurt destroys objectivity, so harsh gossip sounds like truth. Numbed adulterers even accept libelous labels without evaluation.

Fears of social criticism can send an adulterer scurrying into protective isolation. Completely apart from other people, however, a distraught adulterer still has to deal with the worst of all his critics — himself. And he enters that struggle devoid of confidence that he can survive.

Resolutions against Love

"I've failed at love twice; I'm not going to try again," an adulterous woman says, speaking of betraying her husband and then changing her mind about living with her affair partner. Both were individuals she was convinced she loved. Her self-formulated prescription for avoiding future hurts calls for refusing to experience love again.

It's a dangerous decision. A resolution to stay away from love sends negative repercussions rushing out in two different directions. First, such a decision can cause a person to resent anyone attempting to express love toward her. "I don't deserve it," she says aloud. "It just makes me hurt more," she tells herself. The resolute woman reasons that since she cannot return love she should not receive love. After all, in her mind, love just causes trouble.

Second, if a betrayed spouse is eager to experience reconciliation with an adulterer, she longs to hear expressions of devotion and commitments of love from him. Her repeated requests for such statements of sentiment place the unfaithful husband in a real bind. Not wanting to cause his spouse more pain, he would like to be able to say everything his wife wants to hear. However, he never again wants to make a promise he can't keep. He is scared to say "I love you," even though he sincerely wants to.

Eventually resolutions against love may disappear from an adulterer's psyche, clearing the way for openness to a new relationship. If not, more profound problems ensue. Intractable vows against vulnerability result in misery. The steel curtain a person draws around herself to prevent more pain also shuts out joy. True, she can no longer see life's dark side; she has protected herself from ugly vistas. But neither can she catch sight of life's brightness; she has blocked out inspiring visions. A refusal to be vulnerable within a loving relationship guarantees a life robbed of meaning. People who play life close to the chest reduce their chances of misery — but also of ecstacy.

Denigration of Sex

An experience of adultery can radically alter an individual's perspective on sex. The exact nature of the change varies considerably, though — adulterers' reactions to sex span a wide spectrum of possibilities. For some, sex loses any sense of sanctity and serves only a biological function. For others, sex becomes so sacrosanct that they will not even discuss it openly. For still others, sex exists as a disgusting dimension of interpersonal relationships, fraught with more problems than promise. One person scarred by an affair vows never to have sex again, while another flits from one sexual encounter to another like a hungry man grazing among the dishes of a smorgasbord.

A previously chaste woman bitterly hurt by an affair abandons her former moral values for a lifestyle of sexual promiscuity. A man who associates sex with intimacy for the first time in an affair refuses to speak openly of sex once that adulterous relationship has ended.

Not infrequently, an adulterer disturbed by the termination of an illicit relationship loses a capacity to function sexually. Whether it is a matter of self-punishment, confused loyalty, or guarded vulnerability, the behavior denigrates the legitimate function of sex and robs the person of acts of physical and emotional pleasure.

Relentless Guilt

Moral values must be present within a person in order for guilt to emerge. However, ideals do not have to be too high for the guilt of adultery to exact a heavy toll. Increase the level of ethical sensitivity in an individual and the degree of guilt related to infidelity increases proportionately.

Not all the guilt prompted by an episode of infidelity appears immediately. In some instances, guilt grows with the years, only to reach a crisis level long after the termination of an affair. Symptoms of guilt may have been treated as problems in themselves, while the guilt persisted and worsened.

Many people have trouble confessing guilt. Some who carry the heaviest guilt deny it most vociferously. But guilt will not stay hidden forever, not in anybody.

Guilt finds expression in a variety of ways, not all of which appear to have any direct association with guilt. Long-term unresolved guilt can produce anxieties about integrity, prompt dramatic weight gains or losses, unbalance emotions, create dangerous levels of stress, skew biblical theology, generate intense anger, incite self-punishment, inspire a denunciation of religion, eradicate hope, and even deepen despair to a suicidal degree.

Even the slightest reference to infidelity hits a person plagued by an adultery-related guilt like a bomb. A story about adultery in a theater or a casual conversation about adultery among friends sends such an individual plummeting to new depths of guilt. The person feels powerless in the presence of relentless guilt.

Many penitent adulterers have experienced divine forgiveness only to languish in misery because of a lack of self-forgiveness. They appear to be more "moral" than God. Needless but very real guilt erects a barrier that prevents their movement into a hopeful future. Grace has no tolerance for such life-denying guilt.

The goal of grace is new life in the light of God's love. Grace views guilt as a friend when guilt leads a person to repentance, to forgiveness, and thus to a change of life for the better. Conversely, when guilt leads nowhere — when it lies like dead weight on a person's soul and smothers any sense of hope — guilt becomes an enemy of grace. Though grace appreciates guilt as a valuable step along the way to new life, grace seeks to eradicate guilt that has become an end in itself. Grace outweighs and overpowers guilt.

HARMFUL MYTHS

Numerous myths about adultery discourage helpful responses to persons hurt by revelations of adulterous relations. A compassionless posture toward adulterers stands on a foundation lacking in truth.

Grace prefers truth. However, untruths, myths, and even outright lies fail to scare grace away. Grace steps into situations devoid of truth like an explorer entering a virgin rainforest. As a machete-wielding explorer blazes a trail through thick tropical undergrowth, grace flails away at entangled dishonesty, clearing a way to redemption. Grace refuses to allow harmful myths to go unchallenged.

"A person who commits adultery once will do it again."

An employer, checking references, spoke with me about an applicant for a job who had recently been involved in an extramarital affair. "Frankly, I'd be scared to hire him," the man said. "Everybody knows that a person who will cheat on his wife one time will do it again. I don't want that kind of man working for me."

Perpetrators of this myth lump all episodes of adultery into one category and treat all adulterers alike. For a person to whom sex is a hobby or an obsession, repeated acts of infidelity are predictable. Philanderers usually go on philandering regardless of the outcome of any one of their relationships. However, individuals who entered affairs because of needs that have since been met, illnesses that have been healed, or problems that have been corrected are not destined to repeat adulterous acts of their past.

People change. Individuals badly hurt by a previous experience (or experiences) of adultery and happily ensconced in a stable marriage will seldom risk a recurrence of former miseries. Besides, out of negative experiences from previous days, many folks discover the positive benefits of a long-term relationship characterized by fidelity.

"An adulterer can't be trusted."

Adultery has become a major subject of debate in recent political campaigns. Even unfounded rumors or misunderstood appearances of adultery can ruin a person's political career. During his independent run for the presidency in 1992, Ross Perot stated unequivocally that he would not knowingly employ in his business or appoint in his administration, if elected, someone who had been unfaithful to his wife (the masculine emphasis was Perot's).

Without question, an affair represents betrayal, infidelity, the breach of a relationship built on trust. But most affairs are not about trust and distrust. Not every adulterous relationship is symptomatic of a basic character flaw that defies trust. Affairs develop for innumerable reasons. Indeed, some affairs represent an individual's search for a relationship in which self-revelation can occur in a context of love-assured acceptance and trust.

Adultery can no more serve as the single criterion for determining the level of trust appropriate for a person than attendance at an Easter worship service can signal the level of maturity to be assigned to a person's religious faith. Conclusions about an individual's nature require an abundance of evidence related to that individual's life — more information than most people have at their disposal. One fact is clear: a single act, episode, or period from a person's life cannot serve as an accurate barometer by which to judge that person's nature. Adulterous behavior often constitutes one segment of a person's pilgrimage into trustworthiness, not away from it.

"A marriage affected by adultery cannot survive."

No myth more clearly reflects the unique aura surrounding adultery in our society than this one. People expect a marriage to withstand all kinds of other problems. Traditional premarital advice to a couple encourages their preparation for dealing with many different difficulties. Not adultery, though. In the popular psyche, adultery is the sine qua non of evils, the one problem that should not be tolerated, the sin that unquestionably justifies the quick breakup of a marriage, the singular difficulty a marriage cannot survive.

But in fact worse things can happen to a marriage than a spouse's adulterous betrayal. Legalistic righteousness defines fidelity in terms of sexual exclusiveness. But fidelity is so much more than that, and infidelity is such a broader phenomenon than adultery. Two people can agree to keep a marriage intact just "to stay together." Their coexistence is marked by an absence of love, honest communication, growth, laughter, and communion — all the traits that make a marriage. Keeping stiff upper lips, the two people resolve to live in the same house. With puritanical discipline, neither engages in an extramarital relationship. But the couple doesn't have a marriage. Each keeps the letter of the law against adultery, though both miss the joyous realization of the moral principle that the prohibition against adultery was intended to protect — a one-flesh relationship, an intimate marriage.

An affair certainly signals a crisis in a marriage, but it does not necessarily signal the end of a marriage. Following an affair, a marriage can get better or worse; spouses can stay together or separate forever. The outcome is determined not by the affair but by the couple's reaction to it. Couples who respond to the dangers signaled by an affair by communicating with each other better, securing outside help for their relationship, and resolving to give more time and attention to their marriage often see their relationship vastly improve. Of course, it can go the other way. But the people involved, not the fact of an affair, make that determination.

Ironically, individuals sometimes quote words from Jesus to support the idea that adultery should end a marriage. Addressing the subject of ancient Hebrew divorce laws, Jesus once remarked that adultery was the only legitimate reason for a couple to seek a divorce (Matt. 5:32). In no way, however, did Jesus intend that observation as a commendation of divorce in every adulterous relationship. Jesus repeatedly spoke of unconditional love, unending forgiveness, prayers for those who inflict hurt, and reconciliation based on the suffering of innocent people.

"Adultery is a totally selfish act on the part of a person incapable of making a commitment."

Not so. Simple explanations for adultery and one-word descriptions of adultery ignore the truth. Adulterous behavior springs from anger, anxiety, and depression as well as from selfish passion. Adulterous actions can represent screams for help, protests against abuse, or efforts to save a marriage (misguided though they may be) as well as attempts to satisfy self-centered needs.

More often than not an adulterous person is committed to his marriage. "Strange way to show it," you say. Right. But the adulterer usually has no intention of forsaking his spouse. "I love you and I want to be with you," a man tells a woman in an illicit affair, "but I have made a commitment to my wife and children that I must keep." "What inconsistency," you observe. Right again. But a form of commitment is in place and persists with strength.

"An adulterer's spouse must accept blame for failing to provide the happiness that prevents an extramarital affair."

This myth is as cruel as it is common.

In the first place, no person can be totally responsible for another person's happiness. Genuine happiness wells up inside an individual; it doesn't arrive as a gift from someone else. Second, in a marriage, one spouse can neither prevent the other spouse from having an affair nor cause the other spouse to have an affair. Both efforts have been proven failures many times over. Finally, in most instances, a person's involvement in an extramarital relationship has little to do with the spouse at home. Regardless of why it begins, the affair represents an effort to supplement the marriage, not to replace it.

Frank Pittman enunciated the crucial distinction between shared blame and individual responsibility. Pittman wrote, "Dissatisfaction in a marriage may or may not be a joint effort, but the decisions about how to deal with an intolerable situation are clearly individual."[5]

"Once involved in an adulterous relationship, a person will never get over it."

A kernel of truth resides in this myth. However, the promise of this truth is more positive than negative.

Adultery does permanently alter a person's life. One can never return to a preadulterous state after engaging in an extramarital relationship, whether innocence, naivete, or illusions defined that state. The

---

5. Frank Pittman, *Private Lies: Infidelity and the Betrayal of Intimacy* (New York: W. W. Norton, 1989), 46.

change may be for the better, though. A person learns lessons through hurt that can never be understood when all is well. As a result of an affair, an individual may develop a more realistic view of herself, a better understanding of the nature of relationships, a greater appreciation for forgiveness, a stronger desire for a healthy marriage, and devotion to living with tolerance, understanding, and grace. None of that is certain, but all of it is possible.

"I will never commit adultery."

The admiration due such a high-sounding, exemplary resolve pales in comparison to the glaring lack of reality, recognized humanity, and humility in the person making such a declaration. Most adulterers never intended to commit adultery. Many voiced the "I will never do it" myth.

Adamant statements about the impossibility of adultery in a person's life must be distinguished from an individual's honest confessions of spiritual intention, ethical will, and moral resolution: "I intend to work against an occurrence of infidelity in my marriage"; "I am keeping up my moral guard against any temptation toward an extramarital relationship"; "I don't want that ever to happen to me."

Moral resolve merits applause; but ignorance about the realities of human potential does not. Such ignorance is terribly unhealthy as well as extremely dangerous. Authentic morality refuses to deny the realistic potential for adultery in any life. Rather, moral sensitivity looks the realistic possibility of evil squarely in the face and works against its realization.

Students of marriage who know the institution best agree that "love, hate, lust, disgust, envy, guilt, pity, loathing, admiration, dependency, fear, and all other emotions known and unknown" fill all marriages.[6] Given this reality, every person in a marriage is susceptible to the sin of adultery as physically defined by the law, if not guilty of adultery as morally defined by Jesus.

---

6. Frank S. Pittman III, *Turning Points: Treating Families in Transition and Crisis* (New York: W. W. Norton, 1987), 99.

MOVING ON

Grace and truth love each other. Each nurtures the other. In an environment devoid of truth, grace wilts like a plant deprived of oxygen. Similarly, in a context off-limits to grace, truth fears for its life.

The saying "Some people see things as they are and ask why; others dream of things that never were and ask why not" provides a perfect description of grace. Grace begins by dealing with what's on the table, the givens in a situation. But grace refuses to be limited by past events or present regrets. Grace longs for what should be whether or not what should be has ever been.

Toward that end, grace rolls up its sleeves and hauls away myths, attitudes, and movements that hinder truth and healing in an adulterous situation. Once a path to the future has been cleared, grace throws itself into radical creativity that is the true joy of its life — movement toward a new beginning, redemption, the shaping of a new creation.

The Creative Work of Grace:
Initiatives for Help and Hope

The gift that marked my life was the result of the wound.

Sam Keen[1]

GRACE WORK is an art rather than a science. Like a skilled dancer, grace moves to incorporate disparate actions into rhythmic motions; like an experienced sculptor, grace shapes objects with style out of formless globs of messy clay; like a trained painter, grace blends competing colors into the complementary hues of a landscape; like a sensitive photographer, grace captures the meaning of shadows as well as light. A touch of grace involves a finesse that communicates love, a gesture of beauty indicative of honesty.

Grace creates; grace is creative. God established that precedent and provided substance for such a promise long ago. As in the beginning God caused order to prevail over chaos, so grace consistently works for good in the face of evil. Like all divine acts, grace makes possible redemption in bad situations — casting light in dark places, effecting deliverance amid devastation, and inspiring hope in the face of despair.

Creative, artistic grace is gentle, but not weak; as tough as nails, actually, and as strong as an ox. Don't ever think otherwise. Grace never meets a challenge it refuses to take on. The worst of situations tend to bring out the best of grace.

The gentle-toughness of grace appears as grace treats wrongdoing

1. Sam Keen, *Hymns to an Unknown God: Awakening the Spirit in Everyday Life* (New York: Bantam Books, 1994), 96.

with severity and wrongdoers with mercy. Without giving any indication that sin is "all right" or "no big deal," grace picks up the fractured pieces of a sinner's life and with loving patience puts them back together. Calling a mistake an "error" and an immoral act an "evil," grace collects a person's shattered emotions and interweaves them tightly enough to restore a whole. Grace leaves no doubt either that sin represents rebellion against God or that God loves a sinner inestimably.

The God of grace uses individuals to accomplish divine tasks, brush-strokes breathtaking pictures of redemption by employing a variety of caring, careful (care-full) painters. In relation to adulterers, for example, God endows grace with a specific plan of action aimed at redemption or reclamation. Graceful (or grace-full) people then give themselves to God's agenda of help and hope, working among adulterers as artists, facilitators, and creators.

UNDERSTANDING

No sooner does an adulterous affair become a matter of public information than a bevy of people assume they know exactly what happened. Self-appointed critics speak with jocular certainty about the situation: "Well, she finally got him"; "I always thought he was that kind; he just had that look about him"; "The kind of marriage she was in would drive anyone to someone else"; "Lust got the best of them." But seldom, if ever, do know-it-alls know much of anything.

Even knowing doesn't count for much, though. Factual data about an affair tell only half the story — if that much — about what actually happened, and even less about the morality (and immorality) of the relationship. At best, public explanations of adulterous affairs represent little more than a prurient interest in detailing someone else's sins. Understanding adulterers requires far more than inquisitiveness about what they did or did not do. And grace demands understanding.

People get involved in adulterous relationships for a variety of reasons. Helpful responses in an adulterous situation require at least a minimal recognition of the physical and emotional states of the adulterers. Apart from such an understanding, even the best-intentioned offers of help can end up producing more hurt.

Threats to destroy (professionally terminate, socially isolate) a person who committed adultery out of a sick, subconscious desire for self-destruction serve the cause of evil rather than good. To lecture an adulterous individual about the immorality of his ways when that person possesses neither the spiritual nor the moral capacity to make a responsible decision constitutes a ludicrous enterprise. Punishing a sexual addict for adulterous behavior without assisting her in a recovery program to overcome the addiction represents cruel and unusual punishment. And why should an adulterer shaped by a dysfunctional family be forced to bear all the blame for marital infidelity?

Understanding an adulterer requires personal interest and sustained efforts. Unfortunately, most people become so preoccupied with the sexual activity associated with adultery that they devote little thought to the personal needs, problems, and illnesses extant in adulterers. Subsequently, understanding suffers, as do the adulterers in need of help.

Sex constitutes a very small part of a long-term adulterous relationship. To attack lust as the major problem for an individual emotionally disabled by clinical depression leaves everybody involved worse off. To be sure, sometimes lust is the motivational culprit in an adulterous relationship. When that is the case, discussions about discipline in sexual expression are in order. More often than not, however, an adulterous affair points to personal dynamics other than sexual passion.

Grace forces a serious look at the contributors to adultery in a person's life and addresses them as well as the sin itself. Though appreciative of simplicity, grace displays an aversion to denials of complexity. Grace willingly confesses that in the lives of most adulterers far more is involved than runaway sexual passions or a driving desire to sin.

Grace-mandated efforts to understand an adulterer's situation also take into consideration the Bible's teachings on adultery. Start with the teachings and actions of Jesus, for example. The shocking way in which Jesus described everybody's complicity in adultery (Who has never lusted?) disposes of any moral one-upmanship in relating to adulterers. Humility pervades a recognition that any person's dealing with an individual guilty of adultery involves one sinner talking to another. The nature of people's sins may differ, but not the fact of their sins.

Understanding the Bible leads to conclusions that some people find alarming. Sexual offenses stand right alongside emotional abuse, spiritual insensitivity, and intellectual dishonesty as sins against God, different only in kind, not in degree. Jesus treated sins of the spirit (arrogance, judgmentalness, self-righteousness) more harshly than sins of the flesh (adultery, physical irresponsibility). Of course, he condoned neither.

Jesus simply recognized that correcting sins of the flesh can be accomplished more easily than stopping sins of the spirit. Besides, sinful attitudes inflict far more hurt than does physical immorality.

According to the Bible, adultery is a sin, but not an unpardonable sin. People who rip splotches of Scripture from the tightly knit fabric of biblical truth to prove that adulterers will not enter the kingdom of heaven create a monster truth that ultimately will devour them. Consistent application of a moralizing, proof-texting approach to the Bible leads inexorably to the staggering conclusion that nobody will make it to heaven. Nobody! If God cannot forgive adultery, God cannot forgive hypocrisy, dishonesty, economic irresponsibility — on and on the list goes.

Adultery presents no more a challenge to God's grace than any other sin. God wills forgiveness for those who cheat on their marriages just as for those who cheat on their income tax statements. God desires for people to demonstrate this same grace and forgiveness in their relations with each other. Grace is for everybody.

Understanding what the Bible says about the sin of adultery gives even greater impetus to understanding the situation of individual adulterers. Understanding by itself falls short of an adequate response to adulterers, but it is the place to begin.

ACCEPTANCE

Grace accepts everybody, even those whose behavior it finds unacceptable. Adulterers are no exception. And it's a good thing.

"Being accepted is the single most compelling need of our lives."[2] Set that basic truth alongside the realization that social reactions to adultery typically include ostracism of adulterers and that adultery-related guilt frequently causes an individual to shy away from interpersonal relationships. An alarming conclusion emerges: people suffering the consequences of adultery find themselves deprived of the one thing they most need — acceptance. Struggling even to accept themselves, they are sure no one else will accept them.

A flawed equation hinders a general acceptance of adulterers:

2. Lewis B. Smedes, *Shame and Grace: Healing the Shame We Don't Deserve* (Grand Rapids: Zondervan Publishing House, 1993), 107.

actions equal identity (a = I). Stated another way, doing defines being: he did; therefore, he is. If that equation represented reality, acceptance of an individual would signify acceptance of that individual's behavior. Predictably, then, conscientious people would refuse to accept an adulterer, lest they appear to be accepting of adultery. But the equation is false.

Activity does not determine a person's identity. That's God's work. Every individual is a person of worth, created in the image of God and loved by God as demonstrated in Jesus Christ. Personal identity is a gift from God. A person may do evil, but a person does not become evil. Regardless of what a person has done, that person can be accepted for who she is.

A variety of initiatives combine to form the profile of acceptance.

Invitation

An adulterer reeling under the hurt of what has happened, what probably will have to be given up, and what must be faced needs a safe place to be, a place to come and go where the only agenda is being. Numbness, disorientation, and confusion usually accompany crisis moments in an adulterous situation. Affected people long for a quiet space devoid of demands, questions, charges, and requests from others; a place where nothing has to be confessed, explained, or justified; a place to sit, think, sort, evaluate, plan, and rest. Extending an invitation to such a place is an act of grace.

Sometimes a person working through pain engendered by adultery needs a listening ear as well as a safe place. Such an individual welcomes an invitation to talk honestly without fearing reprisals.

On too many occasions to count, I have seen individuals refreshed and noticeably renewed by a no-holds-barred conversation in which they could articulate in someone else's presence everything they were thinking privately. ("I can't believe how I feel; let me tell you." "The joyous beauty of our love affair almost compensates for the misery I'm having to go through." "I want to go back home, but I don't know how to do it." "I've made a bad mistake.") The experience is like being able to breathe again after holding your breath until you thought you would explode — tremendous relief. Hearing themselves speak aloud thoughts they have been scared to translate into words contributes to informed decision making, conflict resolution, and future-planning for troubled adulterers.

A genuine invitation conveys (implicitly if not explicitly) an important assurance from the host that serves a potential guest (an adulterer) as a valued assumption — "You're welcome here on your terms, not mine. I'm not inviting you into my presence to challenge you, lecture you, indoctrinate you, or try to change you." Of course, a host remains true to her personal convictions and expresses opinions when asked or needed. But the motivation that gives shape to a hospitable invitation is that of providing a troubled person a place to be.

Hospitality is another word for acceptance, a term that communicates the concentrated effort involved in reaching out to another person with an invitation to space and fellowship. Henri Nouwen properly expressed the dual offerings of sensitive hospitality — "friendship without binding the guest and freedom without leaving him alone."[3] What a grace-full combination! A hospitable person promises to be near enough to a guest to be helpful but far enough removed not to get in the guest's way.

Affirmation

For a person embroiled in controversy, burdened by criticism, despondent over failure, plagued by guilt, and fearful of the future, receiving affirmation from others can be as important as continuing to breathe. Keep in mind adulterers' tendency to engage in self-torture — putting themselves down as worthless individuals, refusing the lure of humor and joy of laughter, and resolving to kill the will to love and be loved. For such people, affirmation serves as a shock treatment that reintroduces reality or as an injection of confidence that stirs a twinge of hope.

When rightly done, affirmation is one of grace's most skillful artistic endeavors. Affirmation can take many forms. Matter-of-factly stating "I like you" or "You continue to be important to me" works for some people. However, straightforward statements can cause discomfort in an emotionally raw individual and even raise suspicions about sincerity. More subtle forms of affirmation often prove more effective.

A drop-by visit unrelated to a person's most obvious problem communicates an interest in the individual unaffected by his adulterous behavior. Asking a hurting friend to go to a movie silently says to her,

3. Henri J. M. Nouwen, *Reaching Out: The Three Movements of the Spiritual Life* (Garden City, NY: Doubleday, 1975), 51.

"I want to be with you; I enjoy your company." A person bent by self-chastisement and hurt does not miss the affirmation conveyed in such acts. Requesting help that draws on the guilt-beleaguered individual's professional expertise also sends a positive message: "Whatever wrong you have done does not diminish my appreciation for and trust in your competence."

Communion

The gift of friendship is the ultimate form of acceptance. Friends sustain each other in difficult times and share burdens. Indeed, mutual sharing, communion, is the substance of friendship.

The work of friendship involves keeping another person in focus, listening long after you think you have heard everything an individual could say, trying to understand someone else when you are aching to be understood, and choosing to participate in a relationship that involves costs.[4] Friends sing together, weep together, and laugh together. They may learn to worship together, sit in silence together, and make plans together. The key word is *together*.

Imagine the value of a new friendship for a person who has lost a cherished (even if adulterous) lover, the support of individuals who once claimed to be friends, and maybe even the presence and support of family members. Facing criticism and isolation, the person feels that an opportunity for meaningful communion arrives as a gift from God.[5] Little in life turns out to be more important than a trusted person "to be" with.

HELP

Termination of an adulterous situation — whether because of personal choice, rejection by the other person involved, or the pressure of public exposure — traumatizes most individuals. Depleted reason and scrambled emotions leave a person flopping around like a fish out of water, panicked

---

4. Eugene Kennedy, *On Being a Friend* (New York: Continuum, 1982), 85.

5. "So friendship, as a gift of God for the sorrowing creatures to give them a joy worthy of their destiny, becomes an incentive to carry on the works of God in that world of sorrows." Martin E. Marty, *Friendship* (Allen, TX: Argus Communications, 1980), 226.

and disoriented. Without help, the adulterer may make a bad situation even worse.

Grace helps. Confronted by a person pummeled by post-adultery trauma, grace immediately goes to work. Grace-full people offer assistance apart from any conditions. Though grace cares about the future, grace deals with pressing problems of the present first.

"Shouldn't we wait to help an adulterer, at least until she has indicated that she regrets what happened and has requested forgiveness?" No. At this point the guilty person may be incapable of either regret or penitence. Genuine compassion finds expression apart from any prerequisites related to the person to be cared for.

"Well, shouldn't we wait for the adulterer to tell us what he plans to do before offering assistance?" Again, no. The hurting person needs help, whether he plans to stay with his wife, separate from his wife for a while, seek a divorce, or pursue marriage with his adulterous partner. Besides, at this point, what he states as a plan one minute may change the next minute. More likely than not, the adulterer is in no condition to make a life-altering decision without help. If he thinks he is, that is all the more reason to facilitate help for him as quickly as possible.

A desire to help does not equip a person as a helper. Grace as a motivator does not assure an individual expertise as a counselor-adviser. An essential first step in offering assistance to an adulterer involves a helper honestly assessing personal capabilities and admitting limitations. Such a reality check in no way hampers or slows down help, it only changes the manner in which help is delivered. A want-to-be helper who cannot do everything — and who can? — works to get a needy person in touch with persons who can address specific difficulties.

Getting a reeling adulterer *a complete physical examination* is a good place to start the process of help. Successfully negotiating predictable difficulties of the days immediately ahead will require the best of a person's resources — physical and emotional. A checkup either verifies that such resources are in place or reveals needs that can be met medically.

Simultaneously, encourage the hurting person to *see a professional counselor,* and, if necessary, help establish that contact. Caring friends provide a great service by patiently listening to an adulterer's stories of grief, accounts of anxieties, unanswered questions, and requests for advice. Attempts to go beyond listening, though, and begin giving advice represent an extreme (and dangerously unwise) disservice. Securing professional counsel for the individual (and the offended partner) is by far the best policy.

Most needed at this point is *personal counseling* rather than marriage counseling. However, if both spouses — the betrayer and the betrayed — are eager to begin *marriage counseling*, that course of action should also be taken. Personal therapy and marriage therapy can proceed simultaneously.

A heavy counseling agenda unfolds for an adulterer. Patience and tolerance are required as the hurting person works through a mass of monumental questions: How did this happen? What's going on in me? Did I just succumb to old-fashioned lust? Should I attempt to see my affair partner again, whether or not it's over? How much should I tell my spouse about the affair, if anything at all? Must we talk about it all the time? Do I need to say anything to members of the other family I disrupted? Must I tell the whole sordid story to everyone who inquires about how I'm doing? How can I handle this mixture of grief, anger, disappointment, embarrassment, and lack of regret? (The betrayed spouse wrestles with a different but equally intimidating collection of questions that need attention even if answers seem unavailable.)

Building support for an adulterer (and his or her hurting family) also provides substantive help. Feelings of loneliness intensify as the counseling process plunges people into troublesome introspection and heartrending discussions. Often the struggling individuals tend to talk only about what has happened to them and how they feel about it. Each needs a break. Not every moment can be (or should be) filled with profound analysis. Surrounding an individual or a couple with friends who can relate completely apart from any reference to the adulterous episode makes a tremendous contribution to the health and welfare of those in need.

People of grace also provide significant help for persons struggling with the consequences of adultery by *challenging malicious gossip*. Truth is of little interest to a person interested in gossip. Thus attempts to correct erroneous information prove futile. However, challenging the spread of rumors and halting expressions of slander are a different matter. Such actions require only a word of reprimand or a question of purpose.

An individual battling the trauma engendered by an adulterous affair often wants to withdraw from all social situations. She resolves to avoid gatherings in which she will be looked at strangely, engaged in discomforting conversations, asked how she is getting along, and treated (or feel like she is treated) as a curiosity. The longer isolation persists, the more difficult returning to social engagements becomes. Friends do a great service to a person in this situation by inviting her to return to church, to attend a civic meeting, or to drop in at a professional reception with them.

Other needs for help appear. Grace stays tuned and responds with compassion and reason.

FORGIVENESS

Adultery invariably results in conflict, hurt, and guilt. Understanding, acceptance, and assistance beneficially address the first two of these consequences. Only forgiveness can eradicate guilt and thus lay the foundation for honest relationships and a healthy future. Forgiveness means "letting what was, be gone; what will be, come; what is now, be."[6]

Forgiveness is not easy; it may well be the toughest task grace tackles. For that same reason, forgiveness may not occur quickly. That's all right. It's far more important for forgiveness to be honest and genuine than quick and easy.

Forgiveness consists of a process rather than an instantaneous act. According to David Augsburger, at least six steps are involved.[7] A look at each of the phases evident in the development of forgiveness reinforces the importance of grace's creative work in dealing with persons guilty of adultery.

(1) Movement toward forgiveness begins by *once again valuing the person to be forgiven.* Usually that requires a change of attitude, if not alterations in the heart. Immediate reactions to an individual's adulterous behavior typically include disappointment, anger, harsh criticism, disgust, and a desire for separation. Rarely does knowledge of this sin prompt a recognition of how much the sinner is worth.

Only after patient discernment is exercised do acknowledgments of personal value begin to reemerge in relation to an adulterer. Slowly but surely the guilty party is recognized as an individual of worth apart from the values-betraying sin that he committed. What the man did

6. David Augsburger, *Caring Enough to Forgive: True Forgiveness* (Scottdale, PA: Herald Press, 1981), 52.
7. Augsburger, 31-32.

deserves no credit. But the man's entire being cannot be defined by that particular aspect of his doing. He remains an individual in need of acceptance, love, and relationships.

Reaffirming a person's value is not the same as forgiving that person. However, it is a prerequisite to the second step in the process of forgiveness.

(2) *Loving the person to be forgiven* comes next. Both the will and the emotions are involved in this step. An honest recognition of the guilty person's continuing worth often stirs thoughts and feelings of love. Though the pain that an adulterer caused defies all positive sentiments, the person herself attracts love.

Reestablishing love for an individual still does not equal an extension of forgiveness to that person. It does, though, constitute a giant step in the direction of forgiveness.

(3) The third phase of a movement toward forgiveness involves *canceling demands on the person to be forgiven*. At this point, a would-be forgiver looks squarely into the face of reality and admits that history cannot be altered. What has been done, regardless of how terrible and hurtful, cannot be undone. Infidelity occurred. No one can change the unchangeable fact that adultery took place.

Take care, here. Occasionally a person becomes so eager to forgive another individual that a horrendous sin receives a flippant treatment. That's dangerous. Adultery is a serious wrong. Treat it that way. Forgiveness does not require a tolerance for evil.

Forgiveness only happens if the people involved in its development can come to grips with reality and move beyond it: not attempting to alter what happened or deciding to make peace with it, but resolving to live beyond it; not completely forgetting it, but refusing to allow a bad memory to dominate the present and control the future. That resolution completes construction of the foundation on which forgiveness can be built.

(4) Forgiveness actually gets underway by *starting to trust the person to be forgiven*, step four in the process. Passage through this phase of forgiveness may require more time and effort than are involved at other points along the way. Lingering pain sharpens suspicions about the authenticity of an adulterer's desire for forgiveness. Trust is not quickly forthcoming in relation to a person who has broadsided trust with betrayal. Vulnerability differs from stupidity. Ventures into trust must be distinguished from blind risks. Regardless of the strength of one's longing to trust a person again and rebuild a relationship with that individual, caution relentlessly raises

questions that must be answered. Eventually, a measure of trust develops, and the journey into forgiveness proceeds.

(5) At the heart of forgiveness resides an *openness to the future of the person being forgiven.* This, too, is tough. No guarantees exist. Forgiveness must proceed with no assurances that the person being forgiven will not fail again. Temptations come and go. The direction of the future can be changed by a spontaneous decision. Every person — the one being forgiven like the one doing the forgiving — has the freedom to make good choices or bad ones, to do evil or good. Radical openness marks the path that winds through forgiveness.

(6) Finally comes the happy experience of *celebrating love with the person being forgiven.* Guards come down. Emotions find expression. Honest words are spoken. Physical touch leads to emotional warmth. Bonding occurs. A fractured relationship begins to heal. The persons involved sense that the ties of their togetherness may be stronger than ever.

Grace begins the work of forgiveness early, often before an individual has exhibited penitence or requested pardon. That's just the way grace works. God pushes repentance not as a prerequisite to forgiveness but as an important dimension of meeting a guilty person's need.[8] An individual recognizes forgiveness more clearly and feels forgiveness more profoundly if that individual has requested the truth, a question synonymous with a confession of repentance. However, forgiveness need not wait for a sinner's confession of wrongdoing and desire to make things right.

In forgiveness as nowhere else, the creativity of grace becomes self-evident. As Lewis Smedes observes, in granting forgiveness we come as close as any finite individual can come to the divine act of creation. "For we create a new beginning out of past pain that never had a right to exist in the first place."[9]

RESTORATION

Grace enters an adulterous situation with the goal of restoration — restoration of the adulterer, restoration of the adulterer's marriage, and restoration of the adulterer's relationship with God. When you hear

---

8. Lewis B. Smedes, *Forgive and Forget: Healing the Hurts We Don't Deserve* (San Francisco: Harper & Row, 1984), 69.

9. Smedes, *Forgive and Forget,* 152.

individuals or an institution tell an adulterer, "We forgive you for what you have done, but, in good conscience, we cannot help you," know that you have listened to a lie. Grace encourages forgiveness on its way to the complete restoration of the one forgiven.

Churches in particular have a bad track record at this point. Ecclesiastical leaders allow words of forgiveness for adulterers to fall from their lips with relative ease while abstaining from (if not hindering or outright opposing) efforts at restoration. "I have forgiven her and I hear she is a good woman," a pastor says, "but we cannot have an adulterer teaching a class in our church's Christian education program." A chairperson of a congregation's personnel committee speaks to a staff minister terminated for marital infidelity: "We love you and wish you well, but you know we can't have a person with this sin on his record serving in your position. What would the community think of us? We have to protect the reputation of the church." "He is a solid person in my opinion," the chair of a church's nominating committee tells her colleagues. "However, relational difficulties in his past disqualify him from service as a member of our administrative counsel."

But churches are not alone. Employers often feel compelled to paint the worst-case scenario when acting as a reference for former employees who have had adulterous affairs. Grace does not require dishonesty in speaking about such a person, only a statement encouraging a potential employer to look at evidences of change in the person under consideration and to give the individual a new opportunity.

Pledges of forgiveness unaccompanied by a commitment to aid the forgiven person in getting on with a better life represent dis-grace and unforgiveness parading as an impostor. Genuine forgiveness leads to actions aimed at helping forgiven people recover meaning, fulfillment, and even happiness in their lives.

Efforts at restoration function on several different fronts. Grace encourages an adulterer to remain in therapy as long as required to get emotions better balanced, thoughts clarified, and life moving in the right direction. If a person's therapy sessions conflict with a work schedule, grace makes every effort to make the necessary adjustments so both work and therapy can continue.

If an adulterous episode costs a person employment, grace stalks the job market in search of work for the individual. Calling contacts, inquiring about future projects, making referrals, writing letters of recommendation, and supporting a tiring job search are all components of grace.

Grace keeps up with a couple rocked by adultery to be sure they get the encouragement they need to keep working on their relationship. Suggestions about bonding activities, better means of interpersonal communication, helpful marriage seminars, and ways to handle conflict contribute to the health of a recovering marriage. Assurances of the importance of continuing therapy serve a useful purpose.

Should adultery in a marriage result in separation and divorce, grace sees to it that support for both spouses continues, as do efforts to restore as much stability as possible to the lives of the persons involved. Consistently offering emotional support, physical assistance, and spiritual strength creates a quality of hope that can overcome a struggling individual's regrets about the past and fears related to the future.

Grace-filled people who relate to adulterers first in terms of understanding do not even think of giving up on them until the restoration of their lives reaches a stage of completion that calls for a celebration.

THE ULTIMATE SCANDAL

Under a newspaper headline that screams "Sex Scandal" in bold black print, a reporter unfolds the details of a popular politician's adulterous affair. Over their morning coffee, all across the city, subscribers to this newspaper read the sordid story and register their reactions to it with each other. Comments range from a mild "I'm not at all surprised" to shock and a declaration of moral outrage: "What's this world coming to?"

Despite the tabloid's emphatic use of the word "scandal," its news story hardly merits such a powerful description. The politician's immoral actions may sink him as a viable candidate for public office, but his behavior is far from scandalous in the truest sense of that term — a stumbling block, an obstacle, which people cannot cross over or get around. After all, statistically speaking, well over half the people reading the news account while sipping their coffee are involved (or have been involved) in an adulterous affair of their own.

Now, treat that politician with grace and you will have a real scandal. Come out in defense of him publicly and argue that his adulterous episode should not disqualify him for service as an elected official in the community, and then witness the loud outcries of protest sure to follow. Quickly you will see the true nature of a scandal, a stumbling block: "I can't forgive marital infidelity. How could you be so understanding of that scoundrel? Why would you even think of giving him a second chance, especially when he might end up having a part in the operation of our government?" That's a real scandal, the scandal of grace.

Etymologically, the Greek word *skandalon* may be derived from the Latin term *scando,* which literally means "to slam to." A scandal is a means of closing something. In the New Testament, this interesting word *skandalon* brought together two divergent concepts. The Christ who came to attract people to faith stood as an obstacle to faith for many and as a reason for turning away from faith for others. "The idea of offence . . . is the very essence of the gospel."[10]

You see the bind. In the same sense that contemporaries of the apostle Paul found the gospel offensive and the cross of Christ a scandal, many people today consider grace an offense, a scandal. Though Jesus came to elicit faith, Jesus became an obstacle to faith. Likewise, the essence of the gospel — grace — becomes a stumbling block hindering people's acceptance of the gospel. The promise of the work of grace becomes a hindrance to people's appreciation for and implementation of grace. Thus, grace is a scandal.

Here the situation gets really sticky. Prominent definitions of scandal in modern dictionaries include offenses against morals that lead to disgrace and the outrage precipitated by such shameful misconduct. To refer to grace as a scandal, then, identifies grace as an enemy of morality and a source of disgrace. More and more, grace looks like the ultimate scandal.

By conventional measurements of scandalous behavior, numerous scandals surround adultery. Influenced by bad theology and troubled by guilt prompted by an adulterous experience, an adulterer may have grave difficulty relating to God; the adultery is a scandal. As the sin itself disrupts trust, destroys credibility, and ruins the reputation of an adulterer, it becomes a stumbling block preventing other people from developing a healthy relationship with that person — a scandal. The hurt that an adulterous affair inflicts on another family presents major difficulties preventing that family's association with the offending party — another scandal.

---

10. Gustav Stahlin, *"skandalon," "skandalizo,"* in *Theological Dictionary of the New Testament,* vol. 7, ed. Gerhard Friedrich, trans. Geoffrey W. Bromiley (Grand Rapids: Eerdmans, 1971), 354.

Other scandals raise their ugly heads in the wake of adultery. Gossip that pushes an affair participant into an arena of uninformed public conversation aimed at nothing more than passing along juicy information qualifies as scandalous behavior. So does vicious judgment directed at an adulterer. An absence of compassionate understanding and specific efforts to be helpful to a hurting adulterer epitomize scandal in relation to the gospel. Seeing uncaring Christians makes it difficult to believe that Christianity really is a faith grounded in love. Actual efforts to bring hurt to an adulterer establish stumbling blocks to an appreciation for forgiveness.

Yet of all the scandals related to adultery, none equals grace in terms of intensity, controversy, and offensiveness. To get the picture, consider a man or a woman guilty of the sin of adultery. What does this person have to do to receive God's forgiveness and to merit kindness from God's people? Nothing, absolutely nothing. For God and for God's people, forgiveness is a given — a gift. By nature, God responds to sin with loving forgiveness.

What will become of moral behavior if we fail to punish sin? Don't God's people have a responsibility to see that sin gets punished? No. In the midst of a sinful situation, God's people get busy with the work of redemption. Evil does not have to be punished to assure that good will be rewarded. Good carries its own reward, just as sin provides its own punishment.

People preoccupied with sinfulness, judgment, and punishment have big problems with grace. So do individuals more interested in condemning wrongdoing than in trying to help a wrongdoer. People opposed to providing second, third, and fiftieth chances for sinners find grace downright disgusting.

Grace drives legalists up the proverbial wall. Responding to an adulterer with grace does not mean making an exception to the rules or blinking at a violation of the law. Grace doesn't bother with either; it just goes about the business of redemption, convinced that keeping rules and obeying laws cannot be prerequisites to acts of mercy.[11]

Robert Farrar Capon understands the scandal of grace, how grace seems to perpetrate disgrace (to borrow a dictionary synonym for scandal). As it turns out, the good news of the gospel comes across as bad

---

11. Robert Farrar Capon, *Between Noon and Three: A Parable of Romance, Law, and the Outrage of Grace* (San Francisco: Harper & Row, 1982), 144.

news — "the most outrageous piece of bad news the world has ever heard." As Capon explains, "It says quite clearly that, on the basis of anything we can know or feel about the goodness of creation, God doesn't give even as much of a damn about it as we do — and that therefore he himself is no damn good."[12] God's concern is redemption regardless of the circumstances surrounding the person to be redeemed.

Acts of grace flesh out real folly, at least in the minds of detractors and opponents of grace. Their point of view makes sense, rationally speaking. Rarely, if ever, is grace politically correct, properly timed, market sensitive, and popularity oriented. More often than not, grace requires incredible investments of energy, stirs up considerable controversy, and finds little immediate appreciation for its efforts.

Place grace and adultery side by side and suddenly all the scandals that cluster around an experience of adultery pale in significance. Nothing seems so outrageous as grace. To a person guilty of infidelity, grace directs love, understanding, forgiveness, help, and efforts to enhance the future. How shocking! Knowing the worst, grace chooses the best. Grace responds to evil with good.

Adultery sets in motion attitudes and actions that flit and flutter around to the detriment, if not destruction, of all involved. Conversely, grace courageously enters adulterous situations with a steadfast determination to work for the good of all involved. Adultery qualifies as a scandal of sorts. But adultery cannot hold a light to the scandal of grace. Nothing else can.

Ironically (hear the laughter — in heaven, if not on earth), great salvation can be found right in the middle of the scandal of scandals. The grace that looks so much like folly and invariably draws a large crowd of critics offers love and redemption to everybody.

You haven't seen a scandal until you encounter grace. And once you practice grace, especially in relation to people hurt by adultery, you'll retain no doubts about why grace should be considered a scandal — the ultimate scandal.

12. Capon, 150.